July 12, 2015

Dear Homer!

Greetings from the Linnea Bakery! Here's a guide to everything Scandi. ♥. Check out the mystery writer section!

XXOO, love,
Mo & Bri

Kenosha, WI

NORDICANA

100 ICONS OF SCANDI CULTURE & NORDIC COOL

NORDICANA

100 ICONS OF SCANDI CULTURE & NORDIC COOL

NORDICANA WITH KAJSA KINSELLA

CASSELL ILLUSTRATED

An Hachette UK Company
www.hachette.co.uk

First published in Great Britain in 2015 by
Cassell Illustrated, a division of Octopus Publishing Group Ltd
Endeavour House
189 Shaftesbury Avenue
London WC2H 8JY

www.octopusbooks.co.uk
www.octopusbooksusa.com

Distributed in the US by
Hachette Book Group
1290 Avenue of the Americas
4th and 5th Floors
New York, NY 10020

Distributed in Canada by
Canadian Manda Group
664 Annette St.
Toronto, Ontario, Canada M6S 2C8

ISBN 978-1-84403-805-3

A CIP catalogue record for this book is available from the British Library

Printed and bound in China

10 9 8 7 6 5 4 3 2 1

CONTENTS

INTRODUCTION

Why are so many non-Nordic nations currently obsessed with all things Scandinavian? Within these handsomely illustrated pages, you'll find some damned good indicators.

As someone who writes and broadcasts on all aspects of Scandinavian culture – from Ingmar Bergman and Faroe Island sweater-wearing coppers to Edvard Grieg and Goth hackers with dragon tattoos – I've been able to shamelessly indulge my passions over the years, sampling the best that Denmark, Sweden, Norway, Finland and that Nordic interloper, Iceland, have to offer, not least the food; as I have learnt, there is far more to Scandinavian cooking than cinnamon buns and pickled herrings.

What was once a specialist pursuit, I've noted with pleasure, is now a passion shared by many, with a keen and burgeoning interest in Scandinavian design, travel, lifestyle, fashion, history cuisine and culture emerging worldwide. We are now as familiar with stories about the Vikings raiding Ireland for women as we are with *The Bridge*'s barely socialized Saga Norén changing her T-shirt in front of her embarrassed colleagues. And thanks to the Swedish versions of *Wallander* (not the pretend Swedish version with Kenneth Branagh), we know that the short-fused detective's name is pronounced with a 'V', not a 'W'. All things Scandinavian? We just can't get enough of 'em.

Tell people that you are setting out on a four-country tour to meet nearly 50 Scandinavian directors, actors, designers and writers, and the response is, I have discovered, one of envy. And tell them that you are planning to do this not by plane but by train – and mostly by sleeper, at that – and the comments become even more glowing: 'How romantic! Sipping aquavit as one glides across the Øresund Bridge (the eponymous conduit of *The Bridge*) from Sweden to Denmark – wonderful!' Well, yes; but that red-eye trip was as exhausting as it was exhilarating, though it was the perfect preparation for dipping into the delightful pages that follow – and I'm struck by how many of the key icons discussed so knowledgeably here conjure up the spirit of these Scandinavian countries.

I'll be surprised if you can find anything important missing from this survey. Starting with perhaps the most famous raft in modern history, the Kon-Tiki, with its doughty crew comprising five Norwegians and one Swede, we are reminded that it was the adventurer Thor Heyerdahl who set the template for every audacious nautical voyage since. And did the

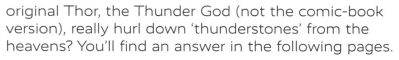
original Thor, the Thunder God (not the comic-book version), really hurl down 'thunderstones' from the heavens? You'll find an answer in the following pages.

You will also explore the turbulent world of the Icelandic sagas, so influential on later fantasy writers such as J. R. R. Tolkien and Terry Pratchett. Also influential, of course, is the violent Scandinavia-set saga of Beowulf, not to mention the equally bloodthirsty trolls – that's the original trolls who waylaid unwary travellers rather than those who now prowl the internet. And have you heard of door harps? Or love spoons? You may well be looking to buy some after reading about them in *Nordicana*.

And the landscapes. Ah, the landscapes! I'll let you discover for yourself the sections on the exquisite beauty of the fjords. Design? Few would deny how dominant Scandinavian design now is (and it's so much more than just furniture). And what about the architecture? There's the aforementioned Øresund Bridge ... and speaking of that, if I'm really honest, the section I enjoy most is the one on cultural and noir icons. The three leading ladies of Nordic noir are celebrated here, of course; dragon-tattooed Lisbeth Salander, *The Killing*'s Sara Lund and *The Bridge*'s Saga

Norén, as portrayed in all their difficult rule-breaking glory by Noomi Rapace, Sofie Gråbøl and Sofia Helin, respectively – not to mention the woman whom we know to be the real Danish Prime Minister, Brigitte Nyborg (despite Sidse Babett Knudsen's protestations that she's just acting). But it's not just actors and actresses up for consideration: we've got key crime writers such as Henning Mankell (creator of our favourite dyspeptic copper, Kurt Wallander); Stieg Larsson; and the current, undisputed king of Scandinavian crime, Norway's Jo Nesbø. You'll also find other novelists who are bestsellers in the Nordic territories, such as glamorous Camilla Läckberg and amiable Arne Dahl.

Reading *Nordicana* is almost as good as making a trip to the Scandinavian countries – or it's at least pleasurable homework for that Nordic trip that you will soon be desperate to make ...

Barry Forshaw is the author of *Nordic Noir, Euro Noir* and *Death in a Cold Climate: A Guide to Scandinavian Crime Fiction*

MYTHIC & TRADITIONAL

KON-TIKI

'Now lads, let's start the engines!' was the first joke cracked on board the world-famous raft *Kon-Tiki* on 28 April 1947, as the crew of five Norwegians and one Swede watched the guide boat slowly disappear into the distance. In front of them lay almost 7,000 km (4,300 miles) of open ocean. One cannot blame them for feeling just a little uncertain about what lay ahead.

Ten years earlier, Norwegian writer and explorer Thor Heyerdahl (1914–2002) and his wife were living on the Polynesian island of Fatu Hiva. One night on the beach, an old man who had lived on the island his whole life told them the legend of his ancestors, who had arrived from the east with the sun, led by a chieftain called Tiki. The tale ignited an idea in Heyerdahl, who started to see a remarkable resemblance between the legends of Polynesia and South America, particularly the story of an Inca high priest and Sun God known as Kon-Tiki. When Kon-Tiki's village was attacked, he and some companions escaped on a balsawood raft that carried them from Peru all the way across the Pacific Ocean. Heyerdahl became more and more convinced that the Polynesian islands were populated with pre-Columbian South American settlers, rather than the Asians to whose continent they belonged. He decided to try to prove his theory by demonstrating that the fabled raft journey was possible.

True to the legend, Heyerdahl built a raft out of nine balsawood logs, hemp, bamboo and banana leaves. No nails or wire were used, only natural materials. After 101 days at sea, the exhausted men reached the Polynesian island of Raroia. Heyerdahl's theories were later proved to be unfounded, but that takes nothing away from the fact that this was a mightily impressive expedition indeed.

LEIF ERIKSON
(c.970-1020)

Every year, on 9 October, American history enthusiasts celebrate the Icelander Leif Erikson, who is thought to have been the first European to set foot on the shores of the New World, 500 years before Columbus did.

Leif was the son of Eric the Red, a Viking explorer who is documented in the Icelandic Sagas (see page 19). Eric kept a German thrall (a person captured but not enslaved) named Thyrker who taught the boy Leif numerous valuable lessons and trades; he was taught to read and write in both Russian and Celtic languages, studied flora and fauna and learned how to use various types of weaponry. Leif was also fascinated by the ocean and listened intently to tales of sailors and adventurers such as his father.

Eric the Red was involved in a brawl in which his opponent died, and as a result he was exiled from Iceland for three years. He took his family and sailed west. He came upon Greenland and founded the first Nordic encampment there. At 24 years old, Leif was entrusted with captaining his first voyage to Norway, and upon returning to Greenland he became restless and decided to seek out the rumoured, but uncharted, lands to the west. Leif and his crew set sail and first came upon Baffin Island before landing on the beautiful white beaches of Markland on the east coast of Canada. They went ashore in AD 1001, naming the land Vinland (now Newfoundland).

These pioneering explorations remained all but unknown to the rest of the world until they were written down in the Icelandic Sagas, and are now celebrated as an important part of global history.

THUNDERSTONES

Not only did you need to run for cover when the Norse god Thor lost his temper, causing thunder to roll across the darkened skies, but you also had to seek shelter from the threat of falling 'thunderstones'.

Ancient legends describe how Thor would hurl sacred stones or *dynestein* (literally meaning 'thunderstone' in Old Norse) down to Earth when it thundered. Although it might not seem like it, Thor's aim was to protect both gods and men from chaos and evil, and these showers of sharp little rocks scared wandering trolls, elves and other nasty creatures away from threatening civilization.

The thunderstones were generally made out of flint or quartz and to harness their protective power, the Vikings would turn the stones into something they could use and keep with them at all times, such as an axe or knife, or jewellery to be hung around the necks of their children. The stones were also built into the walls of houses as a method of protecting the inhabitants from supernatural attacks and lightning. Many of these stones have been found in Viking graves – some of them much older than the graves themselves, sometimes up to 5,000 years older than the Viking who was last in possession of it.

According to the Vikings, for it to be a true thunderstone, it had to fulfil three criteria: it had to look similar to an axe or a hammer; it had to have a 'flaming' pattern (typical of both flint and quartz); and it had to bear evidence of having fallen from the skies, meaning that it had to be somewhat damaged or have chipped edges to be 'real' enough to protect their near and dear.

VASA WARSHIP

It should have been a glorious day of national triumph in Stockholm harbour as the royal warship *Vasa* set sail on her proud maiden voyage on 10 August 1628. The cannon shot the salute and off on her journey she went, sailing slowly through the inlet to open water.

Sadly it ended anything but gloriously. After only 1,300 m (1,400 yd) of sailing, the *Vasa*, which was far too top heavy and imbalanced, got caught in crosswinds, started rocking violently and began taking in water through the open cannon shutters on the lower deck. The rocking of the ship caused loose cargo – including the heavy bronze cannon on the top deck – to roll around and catastrophe became inevitable. The ship had not passed the initial balance test carried out when she was in dock, a fact that had concerned some of the more senior crew, but after serious pressure from the king the fateful voyage went ahead. Accounts vary, but it is thought that 30 men, women and children (the crew had permission to bring guests on board for the first part of the voyage) perished that day.

This regal warship, which bore the proud name of the king's ancestor Gustaf Vasa, had been commissioned by King Gustav II Adolf three years earlier. It was the largest and most heavily armed warship in the world; expensively decorated with hundreds of hand-carved, colourful, wooden statues and decorations. The carvings had symbolic messages and meanings: terrible faces to frighten enemies, Roman soldiers to instil trust in the crew and guardian angels to strengthen courage.

This fantastically elaborate and majestic ship lay almost forgotten on the seabed for 333 years, before it was carefully brought back to the surface in 1961. After 17 years of conservation, *Vasa* was returned to her former glory and can be admired today in the Vasa Museum in Stockholm.

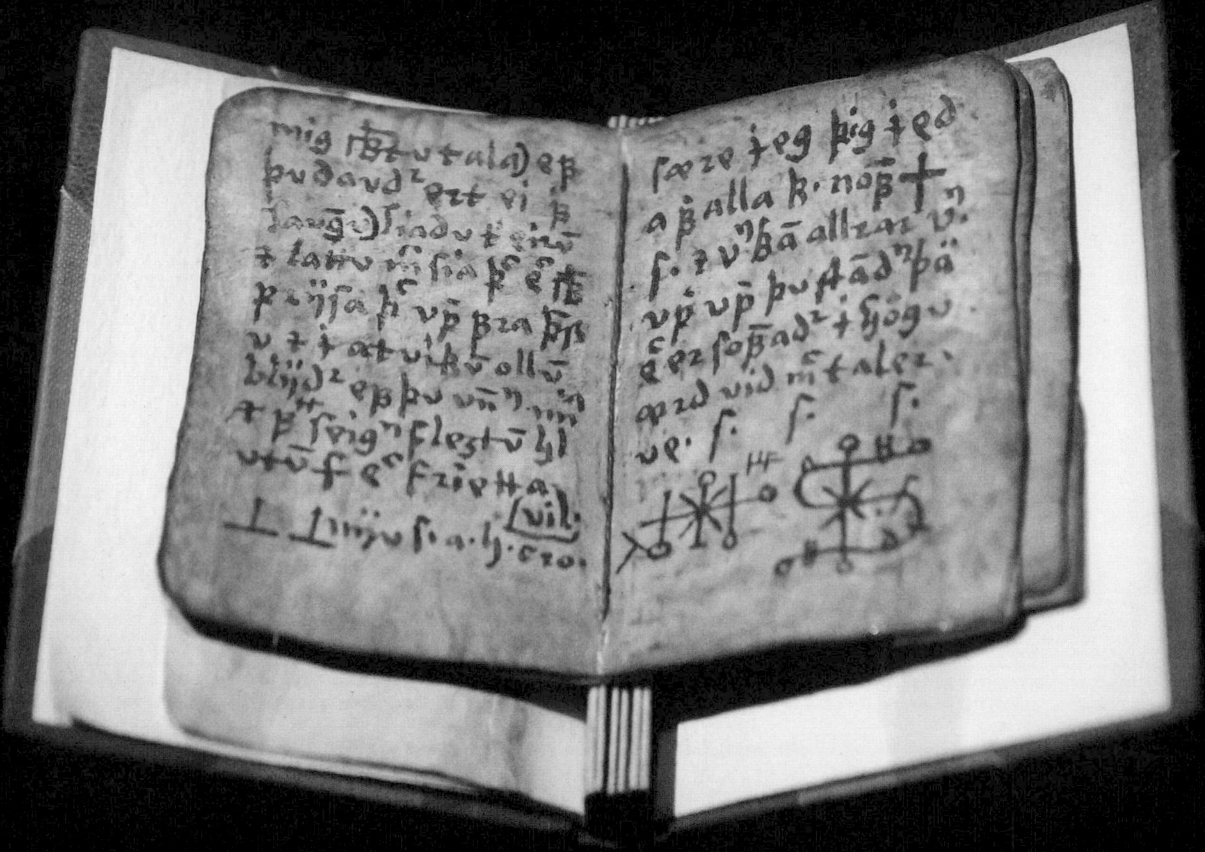

SAGAS

Iceland was not populated by Scandinavians until around AD 900, yet the country holds the most detailed surviving account of Viking history in the form of forty epic 'Sagas'. These stories not only tell us all about the mischievous, vindictive and powerful Norse gods, but also provide astounding detail about what daily Viking life was like.

The forty narratives were mostly written down by unknown authors, although some stories have been linked to specific writers, between the years 1300 and 1400. The Sagas tell us about the medieval Viking farmers who travelled over the oceans to find a peaceful place to settle and establish a non-warring community. Soon after arriving, they were joined by travellers from the British Isles and Celtic influences mixed with the Scandinavian, creating a fusion of the two traditions, although the language remained predominantly Nordic.

The Sagas can be divided into three categories: Family Sagas, Heroic Sagas and the Kings' Sagas. They were written as narratives, which let the reader feel close to the action, and one can only imagine what it was like to listen to these momentous stories of feuds, outlaws, ghosts and trolls around the fire under a starlit night sky in Iceland during the latter Middle Ages.

Many successful fantasy authors have made no secret about the fact that they were very much inspired by the Icelandic sagas: J. R. R. Tolkien, Sir Walter Scott and Terry Pratchett's imaginations were all spurred by these tales. To have a look for yourself at this invaluable part of Scandinavian history, pay a visit to the National Museum of Iceland in Reykjavik, where the permanent collection provides a fascinating look back in time.

BEOWULF

'I am Ripper... Tearer... Slasher... Gouger. I am the teeth in the darkness, the talons in the night. Mine is strength... And lust... And power! I AM BEOWULF!' So growls Ray Winstone in 2007's movie interpretation of the ancient poem that details the adventures of the medieval warrior Beowulf.

The 3,000-line epic ode to the Scandinavian hero, 'Beowulf', is one of the oldest pieces of literature still in existence. The authorship of the poem is a mystery, and although it is debated whether Beowulf was actually a real man, many characters and events in the poem are known to have existed. Opinions about when 'Beowulf' was written also vary, although it was definitely composed before AD 1000 and maybe as early as AD 580, the assumed year of Beowulf's death.

The poem describes how King Hrothgar of Denmark is being terrorized by a monstrous giant named Grendel who has slaughtered many of his men. The warrior Beowulf comes to his aid with 12 fighters and rips an arm from the beast. The arm is mounted on the wall in the King's Hall as a trophy of Beowulf's great victory. Grendel's mother comes to the king's court seeking revenge, and brave Beowulf chases her into the ocean to finish the battle.

They fight violently right next to Grendel's corpse and Beowulf is yet again victorious. He is crowned king of his own tribe, but has to fight yet another enemy in the shape of a fierce dragon. He eventually defeats the creature, but nonetheless a wound from the dragon spells certain death for the brave fighter. Beowulf is buried like the king and hero he was, with all the treasures from the dragon's hoard in his grave, overlooking the powerful ocean.

TROLLS

Once upon a time trolls were amongst the most fearsome creatures of Nordic legend. At the epic battle of Ragnarök (which, in Norse mythology, signifies the end of the world), the trolls fought alongside the giants and all sorts of unearthly creatures in a hellish combat against the gods.

Yet unlike many of their cohort, the trolls have slowly but surely evolved from being a cruel bunch of savagely bloodthirsty brutes, to a milder, less-terrifying version of the legend. In ancient Norse tales, trolls were described as being somewhat slow and dim-witted, but also short-tempered and very large. If you weren't careful they could easily gobble you up, along with all your cattle. They were thought to steal women, children and animals for both their own pleasure and for dinner. However later stories describe the trolls living quite happily in solitude deep in the mountains, tending to their crops and cattle. Female trolls often try to lure human men into their caves for company and it is rumoured that their half-human offspring live disguised in normal society.

While the number of Iceland's 322,000 inhabitants who still believe in the world of fairies, elves, gnomes, trolls and even giants cannot be confirmed (although it's definitely more than you might think), the people insist upon showing great respect for the nature and landscape of their country, and thus ensure the slumber of these ancient creatures is not disturbed. However, one word of warning: modern-day trolls are much better at disguising themselves than their slower-witted ancestors, and should you ever be unlucky enough to encounter one, the only advice you will need to follow is run! Run as fast as you can and don't look back!

TUPILAQ

You would need to be pretty confident in your abilities to withstand strong, ancient magic and supernatural powers even to dare set a *tupilaq* upon your enemy, since, if plans went awry, it was very likely to come right back at you.

In ancient Greenland, if you were at war with someone and wished him or her dead, you could have a *tupilaq* created by the *angakok* (a shaman or a practitioner of witchcraft). The *tupilaq* (which means 'soul of the ancestor' in Greenlandic Inuit) was an avenging monster made to serve as a protector to you and your family's interests. It was brought to life by the *angakok* from a ritualized totem created out of carved bone, wood, tooth, parts of animals, hair, skin, sinew and sometimes even parts of dead children.

The *tupilaq* was always produced in secret, in a remote place and under high levels of security – if word reached its proposed target prematurely, especially if that person possessed greater levels of magic than you, he or she could create one of their own and curse you first. All the necessary components were collected and put before the *angakok* who, sitting in his isolated hut, would turn his *anorak* (a waterproof Inuit cloak) backwards, covering his face with the hood, and tie the pieces of the totem together. He gave it magic powers and information of the intended target, a process that could take several days.

The finished *tupilaq* was placed in the sea and sent to kill its target – but, if one had not been careful enough in keeping it secret, and the enemy had found out, the only way to diffuse the power and avoid retaliation was to confess publically and admit to creating the *tupilaq*.

JOULUPUKKI

Joulupukki is a mythical Finnish figure who lives in the mountains with his wife Joulumuori, surrounded by his assistants. He also has reindeer that can pull a present-laden sleigh (but cannot fly). Come Christmas he comes knocking on every door, greeting the families with his famous question: '*Onko täällä kilttejä lapsia?*' – 'Are there any well-behaved children here?'

The original, much darker incarnation of Joulupukki goes back to pagan times, when the Vikings held festivals to celebrate the return of the sun after a long northern winter. Joulupukki was portrayed as an evil creature with horns on his forehead and a long white beard, much like a goat – in fact *Joulupukki* means 'Yule or Christmas Goat' in Finnish. Legend has it that the Norse god Thor and Anglo-Saxon god Woden would go hunting together on the day of the winter solstice. They led the gathering in Thor's carriage, which was pulled across the skies by his two goat bucks, Tanngrisnir and Tanngnjóstr, meaning 'Teeth-Barer' and 'Teeth-Grinder'. Joulupukki is thought to be a conflation derived from these two creatures.

In Finland, evil spirits were not only said to wear goatskin and horns to frighten people – especially children – into being good, but were also thought to take away presents. The main incarnation of these spirits, Joulupukki sometimes took on a more human form around Christmas, when he dressed in fur-trimmed, red leather coat and trousers. Luckily for the children of Finland, for unknown reasons this wicked persona took a turn for the better over the years, and like his American cousin Santa Claus, he is now thought to be the bringer rather than the taker of presents.

THE YULE LADS

Ancient Icelandic folklore tells us the story of the Yule Lads: rough, mischievous and sometimes even criminal sons of two evil mountain trolls called Grýla ('The Child Eater') and her husband, Leppalúði. Grýla is said to have had up to 72 children, but the 13 Yule Lads are the most famous (or infamous). During the 13 days running up to Christmas, these lads would freely terrorize the Icelandic communities – especially isolated rural farms – threatening to bring children to their cave to be eaten.

The first lad to appear, on 12 December, was Stekkjastaur (Sheepfold Clod), who tried to suckle milk from ewes. Giljagaur (Gully Oaf), who stole cows' milk, came on the next day, followed by Stúfur (Stubby), who snatched food from frying pans. One by one, the remaining brothers joined them: Thvörusleikir (Spoon Licker), Pottasleikir (Pot Scraper), Askasleikir (Bowl Licker), Hurdaskellir (Door Slammer), Skyrgámur (Curd Gobbler), Bjúgnakrækir (Sausage Swiper), Gluggagægir (Window Peeper), Gáttathefur (Doorway Sniffer), Kjötkrókur (Meat Hook) and Kertasníkir (Candle Beggar).

However, as the 19th century progressed the image of the terrible Yule Lads softened a little and they have become less terrifying and a little more Santa-like – both in appearance and persona. Today, children place a shoe on a windowsill in their home on each of the 13 nights before Christmas, and, if they have been good, the Lads will place a small treat in the shoe. If they have been bad, however, the Lads would place a rotten potato in the shoe instead – which might not be such a welcome present, but at least the poor child gets away with its life!

KURBITS

It could be claimed that it was the introduction of the chimney into everyday architecture in the 17th century that made it possible for all levels of Swedish society to enjoy the beauty of *kurbits* paintings. Until then, the small houses of that period featured open stoves, which created an awful lot of soot. As a consequence, decorating the blackened walls was not at the top of anyone's to-do list. Chimneys, however, directed the smoke upwards and outwards, allowing the walls to become cleaner surfaces.

The *kurbits* style as we know it today originated in Dalarna in Sweden. For decades, Dutch and other foreign artists had travelled the country on commission, decorating the halls of upper-class mansions. Local self-taught painters were later hired for the upkeep of the murals and were introduced to the Dutch motifs of large Renaissance vases containing tumbling bouquets of leaves and flowers. They were inspired by these to create their own Scandinavian variations and subsequently offered their services to the lower classes, since their walls now were soot-free and ripe for decorating.

The word *kurbits* derives from the Latin word *curcurbita*, which means 'pumpkin', and refers to the plump and curved style in which the decorations are painted. Originally the motifs would have had very strong religious references: since it was law to attend Mass and the population was largely illiterate, entire Bible stories were often depicted on church walls and alcoves, but, later, non-religious ornamentation flourished.

The art of *kurbits* painting has been passed from generation to generation and today there is a thriving industry of fantastically skilled artists, who lend their talents to Swedish advertisement campaigns, design, tourism and the upkeep of a proud tradition.

BUNAD

The *bunad*, the national costume of Norway, started out as traditional peasant clothing. It differed from region to region in both the materials used and how the garments were combined and decorated, and evolved over several centuries into a proud sign of the diversity, culture and traditions of the Norwegian people. The word *bunad* means 'gear' or 'equipment' and stems from the Old Norse.

During the Renaissance period, the costumes became more of a fashion statement than everyday clothing: colour was added to different sections, the women's dress became a skirt and a bodice, the girls added jewellery to the dress and wore beads and ribbons in their hair, which was beautifully swept up in a bun. The men's costumes were styled after military uniforms.

When the Industrial Revolution made it possible to mass-produce clothes in the 19th century, other, more modern clothes became the preference of the population. Interest in traditional clothing diminished and the *bunad* very nearly became extinct, with many regional patterns being forgotten. However, a passionate and determined lady named Hulda Garborg (1862–1934) fought tooth and nail for the preservation of the *bunad*. She eventually succeeded in reviving the interest of her fellow Norwegians and kept the tradition of these beautiful and diverse costumes alive.

Since many regional patterns had been mixed up and forgotten over the years, a government committee was formed in 1947, assigned to retrace and determine the true *bunads* of each region. Today you can find a wide variety of exquisite costumes worn by the Norwegians with dignity, pride and respect for their own heritage.

DOOR HARP

Originally borne out of inspiration from the Far East, harmoniously chiming door harps have been popular in many northern European countries for centuries. They are especially treasured in Sweden.

About 700 years ago, travellers encountered beautifully decorated, tinkling front-door decorations in China, which inspired them to recreate the same when they returned back home to Scandinavia.

The door harp is, in essence, a wooden box containing metal wires and wooden beads on strings. When you open and close your front door, the harp plays peaceful notes to grant welcome, good health and prosperity to all who pass through your door. It is also said to repel evil spirits. In China, the art of feng shui calls for using chimes around any doorway in a house to usher bad energy out and welcome good energy in.

You can find the most beautiful handmade welcome harps in craft shops all around Sweden, with the traditional background colours being red or blue, much like the colours of the Dala horse (see page 39) – and the similarities don't end there, since Swedish door harps are also painted in the intricate, delicate and ornamental *kurbits* style by skilled craftspeople (see page 29). The harps often have a written message such as the house number, the name of the homeowner or just a simple 'Welcome', as a warm salutation.

LOVE SPOONS

Traditionally the skilfully carved, wooden 'love spoons' of Scandinavia were given as a token of a young man's affection to the lady who had stolen his heart – a way of testing the waters so to speak – and if the lady in question decided to keep the spoon, it was a good sign that there might be an amicable match. It was also an opportunity for the young man to show off his skills and impress the girl's father with his abilities to provide for a future family. You needed to be able to work with your hands in the early 17th century, since nothing else put food on the table.

The spoons were decorated with symbols of romance and affection: bells signified marriage, hearts signified love, a horseshoe represented luck, a wheel was used to demonstrate supporting your loved one, a cross for faith, a lock for security and sometimes, if the woodsman was very skilled, he would carve small balls in a cage on top of the spoon, which represented the number of children he wished for.

The making of these beautiful spoons was a popular custom from around 1650 to 1900, but today their manufacture has become the preserve of skilled craftspeople. Many of the spoons were, and still are, additionally decorated with a technique called *kolrosing*. This is when a pretty pattern or name is inscribed in the wood with a sharp knife, and then a dye is pushed into the fine, carved lines. Originally a mixture of animal fats and charcoal was used to give the decorations a strong, impressive colour.

These days carved wooden spoons are often given as gifts at weddings, birthdays or christenings, and can be found on the walls of many Scandinavian homes. Why not have a go at trying to impress your object of affection and make your very own Scandinavian love spoon? Although maybe leave the balls off if it's a first date...

GATES OF HONOUR

In Scandinavia there is a saying that goes: 'It is better to hurry slowly.' This is as true of personal relationships as any other part of life, and traditionally an engagement could last up to four years to ensure the couple were certain that they were best suited to one another.

However, once reached, a Danish traditional wedding is a joyous celebration, with lots of singing, dancing and eating. A beautiful structure, known as the 'Gates of Honour', is built in front of the bride's family home out of long pine branches, tied or nailed to a ready-made arch, which can be rectangular, rounded or even heart-shaped.

The gates, which are erected either the night before the wedding or on the morning of the big day, are often decorated with fresh seasonal flowers and colour coordinated or otherwise themed with the wedding. To make it extra special, one can add a small, personalized plaque with the names of the bride and the groom at the top of the arch and for them to keep as a memento. The arches can be very elaborate; at winter weddings, it is especially popular to weave flickering lights through the branches to add a little bit of extra Nordic magic.

Twenty-five years later, when the happy couple celebrate their silver wedding anniversary, the arch is built again, but this time around their own front door, to honour their lasting union and long married life.

THE DALA HORSE

There is no other item that symbolizes the traditions and national pride of the Swedes as much as the glossy red Dala horse.

The Vikings were of pagan faith in which the horse played a significant role – Sleipnir, Odin's horse, carried fallen warriors to Valhalla on his back, which determined the horse a holy animal. Following the spread of Christianity from around AD 1000, the church tried to break the power of paganism, including the symbolic importance of the horse. Records dating from the mid-16th century tell of men and women put on trial for carving tiny wooden horses, with which they were accused of causing crops to fail.

The surprisingly contentious, plainly carved little animals began life as toys for farmers' children to play with during the long and dark winter months. However the addition of painted and carved decoration increased the value of the toys, and by the 19th century the manufacture of wooden horses had become a full-scale industry in the province of Dalarna, in central Sweden. Four villages became particularly prominent in the manufacture of Dala horses – Bergkarlås, Risa, Vattnäs and Nusnäs – and it is here that the main production remains today. The Dala horses are painted in a base colour – red being the most common – and beautifully decorated in the *kurbits* style (see page 29) by highly skilled craftspeople.

By the mid-19th century, the Dala horse had become such a celebrated symbol of pride and perseverance to the entire Swedish kingdom that it was chosen by the National Crafts Union to be included in the Swedish display at the famed Paris Exposition. Today the Dala horse can be found in many shapes and forms all over the world, as a proud emblem of Sweden.

FJORDS

Even though fjords are often assumed to be Norwegian, they can be found elsewhere in the world – for example Iceland, Alaska, Chile and Greenland. The word 'fjord', however, does derive from the Norwegian language and designates a long, narrow, deep inlet of the sea between high cliffs.

Anyone who has been fortunate enough to travel along one of those breathtakingly beautiful narrow Nordic waterways, surrounded by high mountains, will have felt the echoes of the journeys of travellers from times past – you almost expect a Viking ship to appear around the next bend.

The geological requirement of a fjord states that it is narrower than it is long and has steep land on three sides. Many fjords are incredibly deep, and it is assumed that they were forged by vast glaciers, up to 3 km (nearly 2 miles) wide, which formed in the valleys through several ice ages. These glaciers were so heavy that, while making their way to the ocean, they eroded the bottoms of the valleys far below sea level, cutting a steep U-shaped wedge. As the ice slowly melted, these huge cavities filled with saltwater and formed the fjords.

The famous Sognefjord in Norway, which is the second longest fjord in the world, reaches a maximum depth of 1,300 m (4,265 ft). Most of the fjords have gravel and sand at their shallow mouths, with a much calmer surface than the sea, making them natural harbours.

There are plenty of enlightening educational tours along the Norwegian fjords for any history-hungry visitor to take part in, offering you all the information you could wish for and a stunning view to go with it.

AURORA BOREALIS

One cannot help but feel goose bumps at such a magical and powerful sight as the aurora borealis, or 'northern lights'. You simply have to experience the 'dance of the spirits' phenomenon first hand.

The Latin word *aurora* means 'sunrise', and Aurora was also the name of the Roman goddess of the dawn, while Boreas was the personification of the north wind in Greek mythology. The aurora borealis is a natural light display, created by the solar wind and the sun's flowing ions, which are trapped by magnetic fields and accelerate towards Earth – clashing with molecules and atoms in our atmosphere on their way. These collisions turn into energy, which reveals itself as the northern lights circling around the pole.

The lights consist of many colours, green being the most common. The colours vary due to the amount of oxygen and nitrogen emissions in the air as these collisions occur. At higher altitudes red light dominates, with green, then purple and blue at lower altitudes, though there are many other colours mixed in within these dominant shades. The best time to catch sight of these incredible lights is around the spring and autumn equinoxes. The lights can vary in strength from barely visible to bright enough to read a book by.

The aurora borealis have fascinated onlookers for millennia: the Vikings modelled the bridge connecting Earth and Asgard after the northern lights, while the Finns referred to them as *revontulet* or 'fox fire' – a reference to an old folktale in which a fox running over the snow in Lapland whips up sparks with its tail, sending them flying up into the sky. The glow was also attributed by some to the shields of the female warriors known as the Valkyries.

MOSKSTRAUMEN

The word maelstrom is a combination of the Dutch words *malen* and *stroom*, meaning 'the grinding stream', and Moskstraumen is a maelstrom of legendary status, situated west of the Lofoten headland in the Norwegian archipelago.

Classed as one of the largest and strongest tidal currents in the world, Moskstraumen is at its most vigorous at the new and full moons. A powerfully twisting whirlpool, it exerts a phenomenal downward pull, spinning round at a speed of 10–12 knots (about 20 km/12 miles per hour).

Its power has been noted since ancient times, with the Greek explorer Pytheas describing its fearsome potency some 2,000 years ago. Later Moskstraumen was acknowledged in the *Edda* (a 13th-century collection of Norse writings) and, more recently, writers such as Edgar Allan Poe, Petter Dass and Jules Verne have made reference to it. However, it is fair to say that some artistic licence was taken when it came to describing the horrors of Moskstraumen, with many of the stories containing terrifying illustrations of large ships, fully manned, being sucked into the abyss.

Moskstraumen is about 4 km (2½ miles) wide and reaches depths of 60 m (nearly 200 ft), which makes it considerably more shallow than the surrounding waters. Unlike most other maelstroms, Moskstraumen is located in the open sea, rather than in a stream or a straight, allowing it to become larger and stronger. Boats regularly take tourists out to see the spectacle, and if you dare to make the trip just remember to hold on to your hat and keep a tight grip on the railing!

MIDNIGHT SUN

Any takers for 24 hours of daylight ... that lasts for months on end? In Norway's Svalbard, the most northerly inhabited part of Europe, the sun never sets from approximately mid-April to mid-August. And during the other half of the year, it hardly rises.

The phenomenon known as 'Midnight Sun' is a natural occurrence in places situated north of the Arctic Circle or south of the Antarctic Circle. The axial tilt of the Earth means that the sun cannot set on these regions during their summer months. At the precise Arctic and Antarctic poles themselves, the sun only rises above the horizon once in the entire year, and then only sets below the horizon again six months later, ushering in the winter months.

Ordinary daylight in these regions is usually bright and white, but as the hours laten this gives way to the soft reddish-yellow light of the Midnight Sun, which is also called the 'Polar Day'. It is a peaceful light and some have recorded feelings of rejuvenation and inner peace after experiencing it. However, constant daylight is sometimes said to cause 'hypomania', with symptoms of over excitement, euphoria or becoming easily irritable and aggressive. However, any ill effects soon disappear after a good night's dark sleep back below the Arctic Circle.

GEOTHERMAL POOLS

When you encounter the mystical sight of Iceland's geothermal pools, with their steaming waters warmed by the volcanically heated rock beneath, you can almost imagine what it was like back in medieval times when they were filled with fierce Viking warriors, dirty and exhausted from battle.

The Icelandic tradition of bathing outdoors dates back many centuries, and a few of the pools used during the Viking era are still in use today. There are numerous thermal springs across Iceland, but perhaps two of the most spectacularly beautiful, called Snorralaug and Grettislaug, are situated in the west of the island.

In Reykjavik – the world's northernmost capital – you will be surprised to find a small snow-white sandy beach filled with locals and tourists on a summer's day, enjoying the nurturing water, rich in minerals that are known to aid the healing of skin diseases – notably psoriasis and eczema. The air temperature rarely reaches over 15°C (59°F) in Iceland during the summer, but this is no problem when water in the geothermal pools is a lovely 37–9°C (98–100°F). Varying mineral content in the waters means that many pools sport different colours, from milky blues to bright emerald greens.

If you are on holiday in Iceland but too far away from one of these natural pools to enjoy their restorative properties, then don't worry – many housing developments and villages have built their own pools for the neighbourhood to enjoy, which you may find yourself welcome to join, too.

ICELANDIC HORSES

Just as sheep compete with the humans for space on the Faroe Islands (see page 90), so do the wild horses of Iceland – with 100,000 animals living alongside only 300,000 human inhabitants.

In the year AD 871, two Norwegian chiefs, Ingólfur and his brother Leifur, moved to Iceland with their tribes, bringing with them their strongest horses. Soon thereafter, travellers from the British Isles, Ireland and other parts of Scandinavia came to Iceland as well. They also brought their horses and, since the landscape was good for herding, all the animals were let free to roam – before long, their offspring created the genetic base for today's wild Icelandic breed.

The small and tough Icelandic horses possess a spirited and individual temper. They are mostly allowed to live semi-wild in herds – often comprising 300 to 500 animals – roaming free and left to find their own food, fending off predators and weathering harsh climates.

The Icelandic horse is a 'five-gaited' animal, with two more gaits on top of the usual walk, trot and gallop than other horses. These were developed over time, as the Icelanders, who relied heavily on the horses to transport them wide and far, yearned for a more comfortable ride.

As the breed is so isolated, the horses are particularly susceptible to illnesses suffered by breeds outside Iceland, having built up little or no immunity through crossbreeding. Therefore no horse leaving Iceland is allowed back in and, conversely, no horses or used equipment are allowed to be imported on to the island to ensure the health and safety of these hardy little steeds.

GREENLAND ICE CAP

The Greenland ice cap, known as Sermersuaq in Greenlandic, is truly spectacular in size – it covers a mighty 1,710,000 km², (660,000 sq miles), stretches over 1,100 km (680 miles) at its widest point and is up to 3 km (1.8 miles) thick in parts. The weight of the ice cap is so immense that over millennia it has pushed the exposed land around it outwards and formed a massive dent in the Earth where it rests. It rises in two separate domes: one to the north standing over 3,000 m (10,000 ft) and one to the south that is slightly lower.

Through archaeological finds, we know that Greenland was inhabited in prehistoric times by several Paleo-Eskimo tribes from as early as 2500 BC, and at least three Inuit-Eskimo groups struggled through the harsh climate of the island before the Norsemen arrived in AD 986.

It might seem a little strange that an island that is 80 per cent covered in ice (and has been for around 18 million years) is called Greenland. It is said that naming the place was actually a clever deception by 10th-century explorer Eric the Red, the founder of the first Norse settlement in Greenland (see page 14). After he had to flee Scandinavia and take refuge there, he decided to name the island 'Greenland' to encourage fellow Norsemen to join him there.

You don't need any special equipment to be allowed to hike on the ice – there are many popular organized trekking trips and excursions for you to take part in. Just wear very warm socks and bring gloves and a hat!

GULLFOSS

Iceland's most famous waterfall, Gullfoss forces the foaming waters of the river Hvítá down three massive curved steps. The river stems from a glacier called Langjökull about 40 km (25 miles) upstream, and the churned-up sediment in the glacial water makes the river fairly brown in colour. However when the sun shines, Gullfoss, or the 'Golden Waterfall', reveals how it earned its name, glowing bright gold as it crashes to the bottom. The tumbling waters produce dozens of rainbows and create a spectacle of motion and colour. In the winter the waterfall becomes semi-frozen, with much of it covered in thick ice and gigantic glimmering icicles.

A staggering amount of water rushes down the falls: in winter approximately 80 cubic metres per second dashes past, rising to around 140 cubic metres per second in the summer. The highest level ever measured saw an impressive, yet very dangerous, 2,000 cubic metres per second.

The falls are today a major tourist attraction, but this is largely thanks to the remarkable efforts of Sigríður Tómasdóttir, who fought passionately to save the waterfall when her father Tómas came under severe pressure to convert Gullfoss into a hydroelectric power plant at the turn of the 19th century. After a long hard battle, she succeeded in preserving the waterfall for future generations of Icelanders.

Visitors need to be very careful when admiring Gullfoss in harsh weather; the wind can be intensely strong and it is dangerous too stand too close to the edge. In the winter, the footpaths can be very slippery, so do be cautious.

ICE SWIMMING

Brrrrrrr! You really need to have your natural impulses under the greatest of control to endure what many Scandinavians consider a normal, and even pleasurable, thing to do: ice swimming.

Since ancient times, the Northerners have enjoyed winter swimming or 'dousing' as it is also called. Traditionally the first step is to break a hole in thick ice, large enough for you to take a quick invigorating dip or a breaststroke or two, then quickly clamber out again and dash into a hot, steamy sauna, if you're lucky enough to have one nearby. This type of fast, invigorating recreation is practised all over Scandinavia during the winter.

There were some enthusiasts who craved more excitement however, and developed the idea (or, for many of us, the torture) further by creating the Winter Swimming World Championships, which were first held in 2000 and attract an increasing number of contestants at each event.

The temperature of the water has to be colder than 5°C (41°F) for it to be considered an ice swimming event and the contestants are required to swim a certain distance in the shortest amount of time. Extreme caution should of course be taken before plunging into icy waters, but the benefits of being rapidly chilled down reportedly include improvement of memory function, pain relief from chronic diseases and stress reduction.

The International Ice Swimming Association, founded in 2009 by South African record-breaking open-water swimmer Ram Barkai, is championing for the races to be accepted into the Winter Olympic Games.

THE SAUNA

There are few more inviting thoughts than that of stepping into a Finnish sauna: that soft, yet intense, heat on your skin; the beautiful smell of wood smoke; the peaceful tranquillity; and the fact that you cannot do anything else in this particular moment other than sit down, relax and close the door firmly on the loud, bustling world outside – for a little while at least.

You would be hard pushed to find a Finnish home without a sauna – either in-built, or in a little hut in the back yard. Even apartment blocks and offices have their own saunas in the basement.

The word 'sauna' is an ancient Finnish word, which refers to both the cleansing technique and the bathhouse itself. The oldest evidence of Finnish saunas are pits dug into slopes in the ground, which were mostly used as living quarters during the winter months. In these dwellings, fireplaces have been found with huge rocks in them bearing evidence that they were scorched and likely used as the first Finnish saunas – anything for a bit of heat in the deep winter snow!

The air temperature in a sauna would normally lie between 70–80°C (158–76°F), but can often go over 100°C (212°F) if you are experienced enough to tolerate it for long.

Much has been said about the health benefits of the sauna, and doctors increasingly recommend the practice for all kinds of ailments such as stress, muscle pain and skin problems, or to flush out toxins, enhance the immune system and improve cardiovascular performance. And it is also very beneficial if you have problems sleeping – all in all an unbeatable and inexpensive health booster.

HYGGE

Denmark is commonly considered to be the happiest nation in the world, and the big secret to the peaceful and contented nature of its people is that the Danes live by the notion of *hygge*. Originally a Norwegian word, meaning 'wellbeing', the Danes have turned this into a fully-fledged concept of a satisfied life. *Hygge* encompasses all the qualities of cosiness, fellowship, simplicity, security, family and reassurance.

Embracing *hygge* means seizing the day and making enjoyment and appreciation the priority of your life: being active, surrounding yourself with your family, making an effort in cooking a delicious meal, visiting dear friends and using your best china – even when enjoying a cup of coffee all by yourself.

Your own contentment and inner satisfaction will transcend through your actions during the day and therefore positively impact on the people around you – it, in a sense, makes you responsible for other people's lives and them in turn, for yours.

Christmas is, of course, the high season of *hygge* when the Danes pull out all the stops, and their best weapon against the long, dark winter nights is candles – lots of them.

Go for a cold snowy walk with close friends, feel the winter nipping at your cheeks, maybe have a snowball fight and later return to a warm, cosy house filled with candlelight, hot chocolate and freshly baked bread – fantastically and delightfully *hygge*!

DOG SLEDDING

Using dogs for hunting and travelling has been a necessity for mankind for thousands of years. However during the Alaskan gold rush of the 1890s, racing with dogs for fun became very popular. Who can blame the Scandinavians for refining this fast and exciting sport to perfectly suit the Nordic climate once they returned back home?

In the 1920s the sport really took off in Scandinavia. The friendly and energetic Siberian husky was the dog chosen to pull the sleighs, since it is perfectly suited for the very harsh Arctic weather conditions with its amazingly soft double coat and strong and resilient intellect.

Dogsledding is one of the world's fastest-growing sports and is divided into three main categories:

Nome Style
The driver steers a sled behind a band of four to eight dogs and competes either in speed or distance. The longest race in Scandinavia is the Finnmarksløpet – a harrowing 1,000 km (over 600 miles) long! There is no differentiation between male or female drivers, and after the age of 15 you compete as an adult.

Nordic Style
Often run by only one dog, pulling a skier or a person on a small toboggan. This is raced over a shorter distance.

No Snow
This can be done running or cycling behind the dogs, or driving a four-wheeled cart. The races are approximately 3–10 km (2–6 miles) and, as with the other types of race, it's very fast!

REINDEER IN LAPLAND

In the harsh winters of the frozen north you will be hard pushed to find anything softer than the warm nose of a reindeer. In Lapland, high up in Scandinavia, howling winds and masses of ice and snow are regular features of the coldest season, but these antlered herbivores are masters in surviving the crippling weather conditions.

Reindeer fur has two layers – the inner coat is very thick and dense, while the outer part is made of hollow hairs filled with air that retain heat very efficiently. Their hooves adapt to the seasons, becoming spongy in summer to provide better grip, and shrinking and hardening in winter so the reindeer can dig through layers of snow and ice to find their favourite food, the lichen that grows on the ground, rocks and tree bark.

In the Arctic Circle, rearing domesticated reindeer is widespread. Breeding, herding and making use of the meat, skins and the rest of the bodies, makes up the entire livelihood of the nomadic Sami people of Lapland, spanning over the very north of Norway, Sweden and Finland. The herds roam free in a unique landscape full of lakes, mountains, tundra and deep forests, although ownership is clearly denoted by clippings in the reindeer's ears. One thing you should not do is ask a herd-owner the size of his herd – it would be like asking for his bank details!

Reindeer migrate with the seasons, and every spring herds comprising from 50,000 up to 500,000 animals move to their chosen calving grounds to birth their offspring in May. They stay there over the summer to build up strength and to raise the calves. When autumn comes, much smaller groups migrate to begin the mating season. Winter is spent in the forest areas for protection from weather and natural enemies.

ARCTIC CIRCLE RACE

The Arctic Circle Race was designed to be the toughest cross-country ski race on Earth, and anyone who has completed the 160 km (100 mile) race will certainly vouch for that. Contestants have three days to cross a magnificent snow-covered landscape 65 km (40 miles) north of the Arctic Circle, leaving civilization miles and miles behind them. So come along to Sisimiut, Greenland's most northerly ice-free port, for the adventure of a lifetime!

The route runs through very tough terrain and, although the race is held at the end of March or beginning of April, the snow doesn't stop falling for anyone. You'll pass mountains, lakes and wild animals as well as experiencing the exhilarating feeling of being alone in total wilderness.

Over the three days, competitors ski a certain distance to reach the day's target and set up camp for the night. The Arctic Circle organization is very firm about keeping the race as green as possible: entrants have to bring their own cutlery and cups and anything disposable is banned, as decomposition takes ten times longer here than in the rest of Europe.

The first-ever race was held in 1998, and every year numbers taking part in this 'winter race of races' increases, with over 470 heroic skiers completing the course in 2014. However there would be no competition at all if it were not for the many local volunteers who pitch in to help to keep the competitors safe, fed and watered.

THE BERGENSBANEN

Norway's Bergensbanen railway is frequently named as one of the world's most scenic train journeys. The highest mainline railway in northern Europe, it crosses the Hardangervidda plateau at a dizzying 1,237 m (4,000 ft) above sea level. The track runs 371 km (230 miles) from Bergen on the west coast to Norway's capital Oslo and, during seven hours of very comfortable travel, you will experience a landscape more impressive, beautiful and untouched than anything you have ever seen before.

The original idea of building a railway between Norway's two main cities was raised in 1871, but it would take 37 years to go from the drawing board to the formal opening day, when the first train completed its full journey.

The railway was laid mainly by Swedish workers, who had recent experience from building a track connecting Norway and Sweden, and at the peak of construction there were as many as 1,800 men employed at one time. The track runs over mountains, through thick forests, past glimmering fjords and through dark, deep tunnels. The surrounding nature is incredibly diverse and a feast for the eyes whenever you make the journey.

Considering the tough terrain, the high altitudes, heavy snows in winter and the fact that there are next to no roads available to bring in materials, laying the track and building the 113 tunnels must have been extraordinarily challenging and dangerous. The workers were paid just 2.55 NOK (£0.25/$0.40 US) for a 12-hour day, so do spare them a thought as you experience the benefits of their hard work, and enjoy Norway as it should be seen, right in the heart of nature.

LANDMANNALAUGAR

Not far from the dormant Icelandic volcano Hekla lies the famous hiking hub at Landmannalaugar. From here numerous trekking paths lead you through the multicoloured mountains of the region, which have been tinted yellow, brown, green, pink, black, white and purple by lava flows.

Four routes lead to Landmannalaugar, but only one of these is accessible by car — the others are far too rough to drive on, and even then the one passable road doesn't make for a very smooth journey (rented cars are not allowed as it is a designated 'F' road only intended for four-wheel drives). The other three paths to Landmannalaugar must be battled on foot, unless you're lucky enough to hire a sturdy Icelandic horse familiar with the terrain.

Landmannalaugar (which means 'the peoples' pools'), is a very popular tourist destination, and from base camp you can choose to go on a four-day trek through a number of spectacular geological elements: the majestic mountains, hot springs, ancient rolling lava fields and sweeping meadows. If four full days in the open air is a little too much, then you can take a variety of shorter hikes from as little as one hour to a whole day. At the end of your adventure there is, of course, a wonderfully warm natural thermal pool near to base camp, waiting to soothe your aching muscles.

You can visit the area between June and the end of September, but for the remainder of the year, the trek is closed because the weather is too extreme.

HOTEL KAKSLAUTTANEN

One of the most spectacular breaks one could choose in Scandinavia is a stay at the Finnish family-run hotel Kakslauttanen. Natural beauty surrounds you, offering endless impressions and experiences, creating precious memories that will last a lifetime.

Located 250 km (150 miles) north of the Arctic Circle, the hotel offers the choice of a 'warm' or 'cold' night. The warmer option includes either a traditional log cabin or one of the stunning glass igloos created especially for the hotel. They look as amazing as they sound and are constructed from a special type of glass that keeps the igloo at a constant room temperature even though the night air outside can plummet below −30°C (−22°F). The igloo glass is specially engineered to prevent it from frosting over, meaning that you can lie in your cosy bed and view the breathtaking spectacle of the aurora borealis (see page 44) at your leisure.

The colder option is to spend the night in a real snow igloo. The dense walls of the icy accommodation block out almost all noise and keep a regular temperature of −3°C to −6°C (26°F to 21°F), however you will certainly be in for a cosy night since all guests are equipped with a beautifully warm down sleeping bag, woolly socks and a hat.

In addition to this remarkable experience, you can go dog-sledding (see page 61), cross-country skiing, take an Arctic Ocean trip, or visit the on-site Snow Chapel and Ice Gallery. And after those expeditions you can visit the bar made entirely of ice or dine in the world's largest snow restaurant.

NORDIC BY DESIGN

CATHRINEHOLM ENAMELWARE

The simple, pretty design of the classic Cathrineholm 'Lotus Flower' enamelware has instant appeal. The soft, curving shapes, the deep gloss of the enamel, the perfect combination of colours and, last but not least, the fabulously symmetrical floral design, make for truly covetable items.

The creation of the range is credited to two Norwegian designers – Grete Prytz Kittelsen (1917–2010) and Arne Clausen (1923–77). In the early 1960s, Kittelsen, a leading artist of the Scandinavian Design movement, jeweller and award-winning designer, was commissioned to create a new household collection for the Norwegian manufacturer Cathrineholm. Kittelsen designed plates, bowls, pots and pans in a bright colour scheme of reds, yellows, oranges, greens and blues. She also invented the type of porcelain enamel that was used to finish each item – an enamel that Cathrineholm subsequently used on all their later ranges, too.

However, the manufacturer felt that something was still missing and that the range would be more appealing if it had a pattern to make it stand out. Against Kittelsen's wishes they appointed one of their regular designers, Arne Clausen, to put the finishing touch to the range. In 1962 the iconic lotus pattern was created and production went full-steam ahead.

The Lotus Flower range was a roaring success, with the combined ideas of Kittelsen and Clausen going on to sell around the globe. Production under the Cathrineholm brand ceased in 1975, and today original pieces sell for vast amounts on Internet auction sites. However, the Lotus Flower design continues to flourish with Danish design company Lucie Kaas (founded in 2012), working in close cooperation with Clausen's family to successfully launch a fresh Scandinavian range of ceramic household items, which all carry his classic design.

MARIMEKKO

From 1939 to 1945, Finland fought three wars defending its independence. After these dark years the success and bright colours of Marimekko designs brought a visual splash of hope to the country. Marimekko has since grown into an internationally celebrated company, selling clothing for women, men and children, household wares, bags, scarves and accessories. Their distinctive patterns are simply unmistakeable since, as they say themselves, 'the colour doesn't yell at you, it glows'.

Marimekko was the brainchild of Finnish textile designer Armi Ratia (1912–79). Ratia's husband Viljo ran a small business printing oilcloth and, since the Finnish state had no money left over from the wars to import clothing or textiles, Ratia began printing her own fabrics to sell. She called her new venture Marimekko, which means 'Mary's dress' (the company was named when it was founded a day after the first fashion show).

Ratia had a clear vision of printing modern, colourful and striking patterns on to fabric, which would promote happiness and beauty in the everyday. In order to show customers the potential of the fabrics, she held a fashion show in 1951, displaying clothing designed by Riitta Immonen, with prints by Maija Isola (Isola would become one of Ratia's key print designers) among others. As it happens the buyers weren't remotely interested in purchasing the raw fabrics to create their own items, but the clothes themselves were an instant hit. Production of Marimekko clothing started the very next morning. In 1953, designer Vuokko Eskolin-Nurmesniemi joined the company and, together with Isola, she provided Ratia's business with hundreds of iconic patterns and products (Eskolin-Nurmesniemi worked with Marimekko until 1960, designing fashion and prints).

KRISTIAN VEDEL'S WOODEN BIRDS

Big or small, chubby or tall – you decide! The chirpy group of hand-carved birds designed by Danish designer Kristian Vedel (1923–2003) has truly earned its place as a worldwide symbol of quality and innovative Scandinavian design.

In 1959, Vedel – who was already an established and lauded wood craftsman, furniture and interior designer and lecturer – created a sweet little family of wooden birds, complete with children, parents and grandparents. Originally only the smallest bird was put into production, but following the warm welcome it received from the Danish public, the whole family was soon made available.

Today, production of these amiable avians, which can still be bought individually, is as active as ever – all items are handmade by a small wood-turning factory in Denmark, which uses locally sourced smoked and natural oak that has been aged for 15 years to create the birds.

The birds' heads are made from wooden globes and are not attached to the bodies, so that you can adjust the direction of the beaks to convey numerous expressions. The bodies can also be turned upside down to create either a male or a female bird.

As with all Scandinavian design, the winning formula lies in the word 'simplicity' – Vedel strips away all unnecessary extras and has won the world over with a product that is the very essence of unpretentious design.

LEGO

The name LEGO was created from the two Danish words *leg godt*, meaning 'play well', and anyone who has ever lost track of time while constructing wonderful new worlds from those shiny, colourful bricks will agree that this elision rings true.

LEGO's inventor, Ole Kirk Kristiansen (1891–1958), was a Danish carpenter whose unassuming little workshop, in the village of Billund in Jutland, would go on to become the third largest manufacturer of toys in the world.

It all began in 1932, when Kristiansen, at a loss as how to entertain his four young sons, started making wooden toys alongside the ladders, stools and other household items he usually produced. When they proved very popular with the boys, Kristiansen plucked up the courage to sell them to local shops. His 12-year-old son, Godtfred Kirk (1919–95), lent a hand in the workshop, and father and son soon became a strong design and production team. By 1934 the factory had seven employees and was growing fast.

With the purchase of an injection-moulding machine in 1946, Ole and Godtfred could create small plastic toys and the idea of the building block was born. After much trial and error, the LEGO brick was launched in its current form in 1958. With its clever interlocking tubes, the brick is today recognized as a design classic.

Even though it has grown and evolved into a global business, LEGO has stayed a strong family business with a core mission of delivering the best-quality products and providing an educational, fun playtime to children all over the world.

SERIES 7 CHAIR

There can be very few items that capture the design ideals of a nation as perfectly as the Series 7 chair, designed in 1955. With its iconic shape and sturdy, yet lightweight, construction, the Series 7 continues to represent the perfect combination of style and practicality.

The chair's creator, Arne Jacobsen (1902–71), has been accurately described as a 'relentlessly creative locomotive', who pushed his way through the Danish landscape of design and architecture for more than half a century. Jacobsen had an endlessly inventive and explorative mind. Unusually, he was able to conceive fully formed projects in his head before putting pen to paper – the detailed accuracy of his blueprints when compared to the finished product is astounding.

Throughout his career, Jacobsen designed houses, banks, official buildings, hotels, wallpaper, textiles, furniture, silverware and even ashtrays. In the early 1950s, he needed a new chair for his studio and purchased one made out of plywood created by the American designers Charles and Ray Eames. This chair sowed a seed of inspiration and the Dane went on to design a three-legged version, the famous 'Ant' chair. The Ant, produced by Jacobsen's manufacturing partner Fritz Hansen, became an instant success.

However the Ant was quickly followed by the Series 7, a four-legged stackable chair made from pressure-moulded veneer. It was this model that would conquer the world of design and has strongly stood the test of time, selling in the millions and showing no sign of decreasing in popularity.

PH ARTICHOKE PENDANT LAMP

Designer Poul Henningsen (1894–1967) created numerous light fixtures for the manufacturer Louis Poulsen, but the one that stands out above them all must be the 'Artichoke' (or 'Koglen' as it is called in Danish). Created in 1958, it has stood the test of time in terms of classic modern design and ever-increasing popularity.

The Artichoke has 72 overlaying leaves, placed in such a way that you cannot see the bulb – which allows for a soft and steadily distributed light. It was originally offered in steel, copper and white, but it was also made in glass for its 50th anniversary in 2008.

Henningsen was born in a town called Hillerød, just north of Copenhagen. He studied both architecture and technology as a young man, but never graduated. A self-taught designer and inventor, he opened his own design business in Copenhagen in 1919 along with two colleagues, Hans Hansen and Mogens Voltelen. Rumour has it that Henningsen's world famous soft-shine light fitting only came about because his mother, Agnes, complained about the harsh and blinding glare of the latest electric light bulbs. (She claimed they made her look far too wrinkly.) Henningsen experimented relentlessly and developed his now-famous technique of creating layers that spread the light in a much smoother and more evenly distributed way – much like the soft, relaxing shine of the petroleum lamps he had grown up with. He soon cemented his rightful place as a great designer with a prototype for the first PH Lamp, also referred to as the Paris Lamp, which took the lighting prize at the 1925 Paris *Exposition des Arts Décoratifs*. He went on to create hundreds of variations on this theme, including the Artichoke lamp.

FIVE LAMPER

In 1925, Danish student friends Peter Bang (1900–57) and Svend Olufsen (1897–1949) decided to put their extraordinary technological talents and fascination with sound together and start a business. Thus the iconic and innovative company Bang & Olufsen was born.

Based in Struer, a small town in the northwest of Denmark, Bang focused on the technology and Olufsen on the business. The launch of the company coincided perfectly with the introduction of 'talking pictures'. Bang had seen some very early examples while visiting New York in 1925 and the pair set about perfecting a system that vastly improved the sound quality in the auditorium. In 1928, when *Steamboat Willie*, the first Disney cartoon featuring synchronized sound, came to Denmark, a Bang & Olufsen sound system was used at the premiere and commercial success was assured.

However it was the release of the 'Five Lamper' (or 'five tubes') radio in 1929 that made the company a household name in Denmark. The Five Lamper not only produced an impressive quality of sound, but also looked as pretty as a jewellery box. Made from maple and walnut, the elegant art-deco object fitted perfectly in the households of the prewar era. It rapidly became massively popular, and, a few years later, it was equipped with a gramophone pick-up arm to play the latest 78 rpm records.

Both Bang and Olufsen remained committed to providing the consumer with the very best sound throughout their careers, and anyone who has listened to a favourite track with a pair of their headphones on knows that they succeeded.

'UNISEX' WOOL-FELT SLIPPERS

In 1992, Pia Wallén's 'Unisex' wool-felt slipper burst onto the market, representing both fresh innovation and a respect for Scandinavian history. Wallén's inspiration for the slipper came from the Finnish Winter War (1939–40) and stories of how soldiers tried to keep their feet warm in temperatures as low as −50°C (−58°F) by making felted-wool slippers to go inside their shoes.

Wallén, born in Sweden in 1957, is an award-winning designer exploring the elegance of reduction. Her personal and professional ambition is to create deeper meaning, sympathy and respect between an object and its user. Her sleek, simple and perfectly executed designs are deeply rooted in Swedish culture, and she both honours and finds profound inspiration in the traditions of ancient Swedish handicraft. For over 20 years, Wallén has developed a range of increasingly popular designs, based on contrasting her minimalist style with a material which, when she set out on her creative journey, was so unpopular it was almost forgotten: wool felt.

The Unisex slipper is made from minimal pieces of 100 per cent wool felt with a textured-rubber sole, and are available in strong, block colours such as green, red, black, white, grey and blue. The slippers are created on the basis of simplicity; the only detail in the design is the characteristic zigzag seam, running along the front and back, which serves to hold the parts together and encapsulates the notion of pure, functional fashion.

HAND-KNITTED SELBU SOCKS

There is nothing more cosy and comforting than pulling on a pair of hand-knitted Selbu socks. The very best are the originals from Norway, which bear a Selbu Rose on them for that little extra touch of authenticity.

These traditional garments originally come from the small community of Selbu, where in 1841 a girl was born who would create a way of knitting that would forever put Norway on the fashion map. A regular accessory for church-going ladies at this time was a pair of mittens, which while warm and comfortable were rather bland and shapeless. When Marit Emstad was a teenager she worked as a milkmaid at a mountain farm, and was, like many girls her age, a skilled knitter. She experimented with adding in a different colour to the knitting pattern, and one can only imagine the congregation's reaction when she and her sister arrived at church sporting delicate and well-fitting black-and-white patterned gloves.

Although initially sceptical, the other women soon followed suit and excitedly knitted their own the same way. It was not long before this way of mixing and matching also spread to other pieces of clothing such as jumpers, hats, scarves and, of course, socks.

Retail production of the socks started in the 1890s, but didn't really take off until the period between the two great wars, when Selbu knitting became immensely popular in Scandinavia and the rest of the world. Today you can buy a variety of items with the typical Selbu pattern, traditionally knitted in black and white, but other colours are also available nowadays.

ALVAR AALTO 'SAVOY' VASE

The owners of the Savoy Restaurant in Helsinki must have thanked their lucky stars when they managed to convince the Finnish architect Alvar Aalto (1898–1976) to design their swish new establishment. Among many other touches, Aalto's now world-famous vase was created to be part of the interior. The design was so stunning and novel that a simple pencil-sketch for the elegantly undulating vessel took first prize at the Paris World's Fair in 1937, before the vase was even manufactured. The win cemented the vase's position as an icon of Finnish design.

Aalto was born in Kuortane, Finland, and studied architecture at the Helsinki University of Technology. In 1921 he moved to Jyväskylä in the Finnish Lakelands and opened his first architectural practice. The young man possessed an unabashed confidence, which he clearly displayed when he had his name installed in giant letters outside his offices. He quickly became one of Finland's most sought after architects, designing many stunning buildings in his native country and around the world, including his most famous project the Paimio Sanatorium in 1932.

Working in close collaboration with his wife Aino, whom he married in 1924, Aalto also took a great interest in designing furniture and fittings for his architectural projects, such as his Paimio Chair and Stool No. 60. Following the success of his exquisite 'Savoy' vase, Aalto created an entire glassware collection inspired by its flowing form. This range consisted of tall, low, wide, narrow, large and small varieties, and you could almost pick any colour in the spectrum and find it available.

Today Aalto's glassware is exclusively produced by the long-standing Finnish glassworks and design brand Iittala, who specialize in forging relationships with native designers and creating pieces destined to become design classics.

GUSTAVIAN STYLE

During a royal visit to the French palace of Versailles, Sweden's King Gustav III (1746–92) was so impressed with its magnitude and splendour that he decided to recreate the opulent style for himself as soon as he returned home to Stockholm. At the time, Sweden's stock of timber and iron ore made it a very wealthy country, so there were plenty of funds for the king to play with – and so he did, but at a high cost to his subjects.

Gustavian Style, as the designs and decor associated with King Gustav III have become known, was the perfect combination of French luxury and Swedish restraint. Typical features were the use of pale colours, large gilded mirrors, beautifully painted decorations on walls and furniture, and tall, Swedish Mora clocks in every room. Also one cannot overlook the lighting, since huge chandeliers adorned every hall and ballroom, dripping with sparkling gems and crystals.

Gustav was at best an unpopular king. On his ascent to the throne in 1771 he seized all power from the government and started a campaign to restore royal supremacy and autocracy, spending vast amounts of public funds on cultural extravagances and lavish architecture. Just before midnight on 16 March 1792, an unknown intruder, no doubt enraged by Gustav's profligacy, hid himself amongst the invited guests at a masquerade ball in Stockholm and fired a shot at the king. Gustav spent 13 days suffering in agony before finally his dying from his injuries.

STOKKE TRIPP TRAPP HIGHCHAIR

During a family meal, Norwegian furniture designer Peter Opsvik (born in 1939) noticed that his infant son Tor couldn't reach up to table level from a normal chair, and an ordinary highchair set him apart from interaction between the other family members. This planted the seed of an idea that in 1972 was to become the revolutionary 'Tripp Trapp' adjustable highchair.

Built to serve children of all ages, the chair has a seat and a foot rest that can be moved further up or down as your child grows – it is even comfortable for an adult to sit on. The point of the design is to bring the child right up to table level no matter how tall he or she is, ensuring that the youngest member of the family feels as much a part of the conversation as everyone else around it.

No one had seen anything like the Tripp Trapp in the early 1970s, and, although it was ingenious, it didn't sell very well at the outset. However, interest grew after it appeared on a TV show in 1974, and sales deservedly soared.

Opsvik designed the chair for the Norwegian company Stokke, founded in 1932, which is a business with strong ethical views: they not only create smart, safe and comfortable solutions that further children's development and growth, but also place emphasis on caring for the planet that these children will inherit from us. The original chair was made out of beech, but nowadays you can find it in plenty of finishes and a wide array of colours with bright, detachable cushions to add to the comfort.

FAROE ISLE JUMPER

The Faroe Isle archipelago is a small group of 18 islands, situated between the Norwegian Sea and the North Atlantic Ocean – halfway between Iceland and Norway. Approximately 50,000 people live on these ancient islands, almost in danger of being crowded out by over 70,000 fluffy Faroe sheep with which the islanders share the land.

It has been suggested that the name 'Faroe' derives from the Old Norse words for 'sheep island', and it's certainly true that these wonderfully woolly animals form the basis of a healthy knitwear industry, which was originally borne out of the necessity of keeping warm during the winter. The islanders' particular style of knitwear and pattern combination has slowly but surely evolved from practical workwear into an unmistakable fashion statement.

The wool from the hardy Faroe Isle sheep has a high lanolin content to it, which makes it both warm and somewhat water resistant. Beautifully snug scarves, gloves and, most famously, jumpers are knitted – all handmade and carrying the distinctive Nordic patterns in multiple colours – by the local women passing down traditions from generation to generation.

Recently the Faroe Isles' knitwear industry has enjoyed a well-deserved boost following the media attention garnered by the cosy, yet practical, jumpers of Detective Sarah Lund in the Danish TV series *The Killing* (see page 126). The Faroese design team Guðrun & Guðrun created Lund's celebrated sweaters (a different one for each of the three series). Founded by Guðrun Ludvig and Guðrun Rogvadottir in 2007, Guðrun & Guðrun has since grown into an international name with a wide range of products, proudly stocked by famous department stores such as Harrods in London.

HUMMEL HI-TOPS

Around the world you will find people wearing ingenious and ever-cool Hummel footwear, whether they are playing basketball, handball, volleyball, rugby, shinty, futsal, innebandy or football – or no sport at all. In 90 years Hummel has grown from a simple sports shoe manufacturer to a popular fashion brand. Their best-known shoe is the hi-top emblazoned with the company's double-chevron and, since retro wear never goes out of style, they are likely to keep on growing.

The company began life one day in 1923, when German shoemaker Albert Messmer stood in the pouring rain watching a football match. He saw the players slipping and sliding in the mud and had a 'eureka' moment: he was going to make football shoes with cleats. Cleats are studs attached to the sole of the shoe, giving the player a stronger, safer grip. Other shoemakers were already experimenting with cleats, but Messmer was determined to make his better.

Messmer and his brother started a business in the same year, naming it Hummel (the German for 'bumblebee'). Business went well at first, but the brothers sadly had to file for bankruptcy in 1935. Over the years Hummel passed through many hands, but became 100 per cent Danish in 1980. In 1999, the company was bought by the Danish entrepreneur Christian Stadil, who instigated the brand's slogan, 'Change the world through sport'. Today Hummel strives to make the world a better place by using recycled materials in their products, and supporting various 'karma' projects for children and young people in war-torn and unsettled countries.

SWEDISH HASBEENS

Looking at a Swedish clog or *träsko*, you might be fooled into thinking that they are the most uncomfortable pieces of footwear in the world, but they really aren't! Once you let your foot relax and allow it to nestle in the firm, wooden heel, snugly held by the sturdy leather upper, you will likely never want to take them off again.

There are plenty of varieties of wooden-soled shoes available today, but you just can't beat a properly made, genuine Swedish clog. This was the opinion of Swedish Emy Blixt, who happened to come across a large quantity of clogs and bags from the 1970s in the basement of a closed-down shoe factory near her home. Blixt had a strong sentimental streak and couldn't just leave them there to be forgotten – she herself had grown up wearing clogs, along with every man, woman and child that she knew. Yet they had somehow faded in popularity, and so Blixt made it her mission to change the modest clog's fortunes: Swedish Hasbeens was born.

In the summer of 2006, Blixt started a business with her childhood friend, Cilla Wingård Neumann, with the intention of bringing Swedish Hasbeens to market. The shoes were an instant success, and today they sell in shops the world over, with production still mostly based in Sweden.

The range has expanded and now includes bags and belts, along with a large range of fantastically comfortable shoes, boots and sandals available in all sorts of colours and shapes. However, all retain the distinct, classic look of the Swedish Hasbeens style.

ILSE JACOBSON RUBBER BOOTS

Just north of the Danish capital Copenhagen lies the idyllic seaside town of Hornbæk, which has been a source of inspiration for many of the famous artists and creative minds of the Nordic territories. This is certainly true of Danish shoe designer Ilse Jacobsen, who finds it an invaluable source of creativity and feels very much at home there.

While always having been creative, Jacobsen did not originally intend to go into fashion, and chose to study political science and economics at university. After finishing her degree, she returned to her beloved Hornbæk and opened a restaurant. Fate was to have a different plan for Jacobsen, however, and a friend of hers who ran a shoe shop asked if she wanted to take over the business. After a few years of selling shoes made by others, Jacobsen came to the conclusion that she also had a lot to offer the footwear business and launched her own brand, 'Ilse Jacobsen Hornbæk', in 1993.

Jacobsen's mission is to offer the consumer the best-quality design and materials, inspired by her Scandinavian rural roots and surroundings. She strives to give the customer something comfortable yet still attractive. The range today includes clothing and accessories as well as shoes.

Jacobsen's undisputed bestseller is the lace-up rubber boot – a favourite of women all over the world. The boots are made from 100 per cent natural rubber and are padded with a very cosy cotton fleece. You can also purchase a specially designed inner-sock, which makes them even more snug in winter! All are made by hand and each pair takes three months to create from start to finish. The iconic laces on the front perfectly complete the picture.

ACNE PISTOL BOOTS

Want to look sharp? Then pull on a pair of Acne's bestselling 'Pistol' boots! With its distinctive zip and thick heel, the ankle boot is a snappy mixture of motorcycle and cowboy boot. Countless copies have been made, but none can compete with the stylish originals.

Acne started out in 1996 when creative director Jonny Johansson and three friends laid the foundations for what was to become a worldwide phenomenon. In 1997 the company exploded on to the scene when Johansson sewed 100 pairs of straight-legged denim jeans with bright red stitching and gave them away to friends, family and a few fashion insiders. As luck would have it, the jeans were picked up both by *Vogue* Paris and *Wallpaper** magazine.

'I wish we hadn't called it that...', Johansson once said about the fashion brand's unusual name, but the team stuck with it, later becoming Acne Studio. The letters stand for the company's vision: 'Ambition to Create Novel Expression', an aesthetic that is reflected in many of the brand's products. Johansson is very much inspired by music, literature, art, photography and design, and in Acne's futuristically clinical-looking stores you can find a fabulous mixture of things to purchase: magazines, books, footwear, accessories, furniture and both men's and women's ready-to-wear clothing. The company often collaborates with established designers, artists and craftspeople to create exclusive limited editions and to produce exhibitions in their stores in all the major fashion capitals, including London, Paris, Stockholm, New York and Tokyo.

MALENE BIRGER

When MTV Europe crowns you the 'Queen of Fashion in Copenhagen' you can safely say that you have arrived, and Malene Birger (born in 1962) has done just that. In 2011, as a celebration of Danish design, a sketch for one of her dresses was featured on a special-edition stamp and Birger was immortalized as one of Denmark's finest contributors to modern fashion.

Her signature style is a divine mixture of bold colours, prints and patterns, paired with monochromes and block colours, while her use of fabric and drapery creates a very feminine silhouette. Birger's clothes are elegant yet easy to wear and she counts Helena Christensen, *Borgen*'s Sidse Babett Knudsen (see page 167) and Sofie Gråbøl of *The Killing* (see page 138) among her celebrity fans. She is also beloved by Royal households around the world, with Catherine, Duchess of Cambridge, Crown Princess Victoria of Sweden and Crown Princess Mary of Denmark often seen wearing her creations.

Having won several awards while working as the head designer for other clothing companies, by the mid 1990s Birger felt that she was ready to stand on her own two feet. In 1997 she co-founded her first company, Day Birger et Mikkelsen, with business partner Keld Mikkelsen. In February of 2003 Birger launched her own label 'By Malene Birger'. Birger's way of working is, in her own words, 'sticking with her gut feeling on designs' and she admits she 'does not compromise'; these ground rules are clearly successful since the label is now stocked in over 40 countries. In 2010, Birger sold the 'By...' label and stepped down as creative director to focus on her latest homeware venture, Birger No.1962, and continue her work as an ambassador for UNICEF.

SANDQVIST BACKPACK

Anton Sandqvist, an international high-flyer with a thriving career in an electronics company, found that he was stacking up a massive 100 travel days every year and stopped to take a long, hard look at his life. Something was missing and he soon knew what it was – he yearned to do something creative. In the autumn of 2004, Sandqvist found an industrial sewing machine on the internet, installed it in his cellar, and sat down to start work on a bag for himself.

His main inspiration came from the Swiss brand Freitag's messenger bags, and, 30 hours of hard work later, Sandquist had created his first product. He received a number of compliments on it, approached some stockists and soon a small retail production started. Along with his brother Daniel and schoolfriend Sebastian Westin, Anton nurtured the business, and saw it go from strength to strength, ultimately having to move production to China. In 2007, the first complete collection of bags for men was launched, which was well received at the Copenhagen International Fashion Fair and international orders rolled in.

While reading a book about Norwegian explorer Roald Amundsen, Sandqvist was inspired to create a backpack and developed one in canvas and leather. The bag became a huge hit and Sandqvist developed a number of backpack designs that are now a substantial part of the range. Today the company also produces bags and other accessories for women and children and is a Swedish design force to be reckoned with.

EATING &
MAKING
MERRY

MIDSUMMER CELEBRATIONS

The Scandinavian Midsummer's Eve is filled to the brim with magic and mystery, and should be spent barefoot in high, soft grass – dancing outdoors to traditional music surrounded by dear friends and family.

Midsummer festivities are centred around the summer solstice (the longest day of the year), which in the northern hemisphere will fall on either 21 or 22 June, depending on shifts in the calendar. Midsummer was originally a pagan holiday, celebrating the fertility of the land and wishing for a good harvest, and many rituals and customs were associated with these festivities. The houses were decorated with handmade wreaths and garlands, both inside and out, to signify productivity and fertility and huge bonfires were lit to scare away malicious and evil spirits, who were believed to roam the countryside around midsummer time, along with a whole lot of nasty witches.

Nowadays we celebrate in a less fearful manner, and, as with most Scandinavian celebrations, food and music take centre stage. Long tables are draped with white tablecloths, delicious food is served in abundance and a traditional maypole is erected and decorated with fresh flowers. Guests come in their finest national costumes and the band plays folk dances such as *schottis*, mazurka, polka, *snoa*, waltz and *hambo*, danced by old and young late into the night.

It is said that if a young girl picks a bouquet of seven different types of summer flowers in total silence, jumps over seven stone walls, then places the bouquet under her pillow on this very night, she will dream of her one true love.

PICKLED HERRING

To put a Scandinavian slant on a well-known saying, 'all herring shall swim thrice – once in the ocean, once in vinegar and then, lastly, in the aquavit that we drink to accompany them'!

The Swedish love of herring cannot be understated, and seems to have started around AD 1000 in the south of the country. Herring fishing was one of the easiest jobs a man could have, thanks to an abundance of incredibly dense shoals – some up to 10 km (6 miles) long and containing hundreds of millions of fish. Many tales were told of the difficulty of rowing a boat through the teaming waters, or of herring leaping into the boat and filling it all on their own without any need for actual fishing. With such a vast quantity of fish available it was necessary to bring in pickling techniques to allow for storage or transportation.

Over the centuries, however, pickled herring made a spectacular journey from being disregarded as 'poor man's feed' to becoming a treasured and celebrated national dish when it was discovered by the upper classes in the mid-15th century. Since then pickled herring, or *inlagd sill,* has become the essential centrepiece to any self-respecting *smörgåsbord* (see page 121). Indeed, the current Swedish king, Carl XVI Gustaf, is apparently an enthusiastic master in pickling herrings and, it is said, happily shares his opinions on the matter with the royal head chef.

'The silver of the ocean and the gold of the palate' is the slogan of Skånska Sillaacademien (the Skåne Herring Academy), an enthusiastic group of herring lovers in southern Sweden who devote their time to preserving, developing and promoting the pickled herring. The society holds large feasts – where guests can try out new recipes and to learn about their heritage – and also organizes conferences outside Scandinavia. No doubt many a hesitant novice has been converted to the way of the herring thanks to this dedicated bunch!

LINGONBERRIES

There is nothing more majestic than stepping into a tall, deep, dark Scandinavian forest, where the ground is lush with the wonderful softness of layers and layers of vegetation lying under your feet. The intense aroma seems to conjure up ancient memories and hits you right in the heart... So grab your basket, because we're going lingonberry picking!

Considering that northern winters are very long and cold, and the summers relatively short, the lingonberry is the ideal fruit for this region. This low-growing evergreen bush can withstand chills of up to −40°C (−40°F) and bears plentiful small red berries during the months of August and September. Lingonberry shrubs thrive in the acidic soil of the pine forest, so it's off to the woods we go if we want to make our favourite jam, jelly or juice.

The berries are full of benzoic acid, which acts as a natural preservative ensuring a long shelf life for produce made from them – even with low amounts of sugar added. The berries are full of vitamins and minerals and are also used as a common and very effective remedy for urinary tract infection.

We love our lingonberries in all manner of preparations, but it's especially popular as a juice drink (*lingonsaft*) or preserve (*lingonsylt*) to accompany traditional meatballs (see page 111). In Scandinavia, the lingonberry makes a regular appearance at many meals, from modest home-cooked suppers to royal weddings.

BRENNIVÍN

The name *brennivín* in Icelandic means 'burning wine'. All the Scandinavian countries have an equivalent to it, but none of them has anywhere near the potency of 'The Black Death' or 'Devil's Brew' as it is also known (there's a Nordic saying, 'a dear child has many names...').

Brennivín is Iceland's signature drink and, although many natives today dare not touch it themselves, it would have been customary to have a swig of it when feeling particularly patriotic in pagan times, especially during Þorrablót, which was a sacrificial festival of offerings to the Norse god Thor (or 'Þórr' in Icelandic) in mid-January. The celebration is still observed today, although with a lot less livestock being sacrificed, thankfully. Plenty of food and drink is on the menu at these festivities, and the one thing you cannot do without at this annual event is *brennivín*, standing proud with a practically hallucinogenic 80 per cent alcohol content when bottled.

Either fermented grains or potato mash form the base for *brennivín* and it is flavoured mainly with botanical ingredients such as angelica, caraway and cumin. The herbs are steeped in the alcohol for a long period of time to extract as much of the flavour as possible.

Brennivín should be enjoyed well chilled in small shot glasses, and to complete the flavoursome treat, it should traditionally be drunk in accompaniment to *hákarl* – the uniquely Icelandic dish of fermented shark meat.

WILD STRAWBERRIES

For many Scandinavians, the very best summer childhood memory is that of sneaking out in the still-wet grass, far too early on a summer's morning to loot the wild-strawberry patch of all its ruby-red treasures.

Before the garden strawberry (the larger variety that we're now more familiar with) was introduced, wild strawberries were widely cultivated, but now they are only grown in small amounts for gourmet purposes. The wild berries are very small, but absolutely full of flavour.

The plants require very little attention and multiply by growing long stolons (over-ground runners) that create new plants. The wild strawberries prefer not to be planted too deep and like a sunny and peaceful spot to grow in. Given these conditions, they will happily provide you with delicate and tasty little red berries all summer long. If one feels adventurous, there are also yellow, white and green varieties to try out. The colour develops first, just before the berries ripen fully, so don't be tempted to harvest too soon!

Scandinavians recognize that there is something very special about wild strawberries – it is as if their size and their comparative rarity make them a little bit magical. The simple pleasure of peering down to find tiny red berries hiding under the large, dark leaves instils a childlike feeling of joy in even the most cynical of adults.

MEATBALLS

Travelling through any of the Scandinavian countries, it is evident that the tradition of eating meatballs as part of a morning, noon or evening meal is well and truly alive, with no sign of their popularity declining. These small balls – which should be no more than 2.5 cm (1 in) across – are traditionally made from an evenly measured mixture of minced beef and pork, but you could be lucky enough to discover them made from veal, deer, wild boar, reindeer or even moose.

In Denmark they are called *frikadeller*, in Finland *lihapullat*, in Norway *kjøttboller*, in Iceland *kjötbollur* and, finally, in Sweden they are known as *köttbullar*. It was Swedish King Charles XII, held in exile in the Ottoman Empire in the early 18th century, who discovered the recipe there and brought it back with him to the North.

The meatballs are made by combining the beef and pork mince, finely chopped fresh or fried onion, breadcrumbs soaked in milk, an egg, sea salt, white pepper and a pinch of allspice – no more, no less. Fry the meatballs in butter until they are browned evenly on all sides and cooked though, and serve with freshly made mashed potato, homemade lingonberry preserve (see page 106) and pickled sweet cucumber. However the dish is not complete without the addition of a wonderfully flavoursome gravy made by mixing the savoury pan juices with a dash or three of cream, seasoned to taste. Delicious!

SKYR

The words *Streptococcus salivarius* ssp. *thermophilus* and *Lactobacillus delbrueckii* ssp. *bulgaricus* don't immediately suggest a refreshing and delicious midday snack to most of us, but to the people of Iceland they most certainly do.

These bacteria are two of the key components in Iceland's most beloved dairy delicacy: *skyr*. It is most likely that it was the Norwegian Vikings who brought their knowledge of the preservation techniques involved in making *skyr* with them as they came from across the seas. When they had finished killing, burning and pillaging they settled, and eventually shared their knowledge with the northern island natives.

Skyr does bear a resemblance to thick, creamy yoghurt but is in fact a type of fresh cheese. It has a slightly sour taste to it with an almost hidden hint of residual sweetness. Traditionally *skyr* should be made using unpasteurized milk – many Icelanders would still refuse to use anything else – but as we have progressed into more health-conscious traditions, nowadays it has to be made with pasteurized milk if it is to be sold commercially.

Skyr has a very low fat content – next to none, in fact – and contains exceptional levels of calcium and protein, which makes it the ideal food for active people. The rest of us, however, since it is so low in calories, can add a sprinkle of cinnamon sugar and an accompanying flatbread almost guilt-free. This nourishing dish is surely a contributing factor to Icelanders being the longest-living nation in Europe!

KARJALANPIIRAKKA

Finland, the country of a thousand lakes and endless forests, lies neatly between Russia and Sweden and boasts a cuisine full of rural country dishes from the east and more modern influences from the west. The consequence of this is a fascinating mixture of hearty and nurturing wholesome foods, which display strong links to a multicultural past.

As World War II raged in central and northern Europe, great swathes of the Finnish region Northern Karelia was used as a battleground, resulting in many Karelians fleeing into other parts of the country. In the process, they brought with them their local traditions and rustic recipes; the most famous one being the pastry called *karjalanpiirakka*.

It takes a bit of time to make these mouth-watering pies or pasties, but anyone who has ever made them is aware that it is well worth the effort. Traditionally they are made from rye dough, which is rolled out thinly into an oval shape, then filled with very thick rice porridge that has been cooked for at least 45 minutes. The sides of the dough are rolled up towards the centre and pinched together, then the pasties are baked in a hot oven for 25–30 minutes until thoroughly cooked through and crispy.

To top it off, and to really enjoy a *piirakka* in the most authentic way, you should make a mixture of creamed butter and chopped boiled eggs called *munavoi* – add this to the pasties and you have a big tasty bite of true northern tradition.

NOMA

Noma, a combination of the words *nordisk* (Nordic) and *mad* (food), was the brainchild of Claus Meyer (born in 1963), an internationally renowned cookery author, TV personality, entrepreneur and professor who, in late 2002, had the idea of opening a restaurant that would serve mainly Nordic and local ingredients.

René Redzepi (born in 1977) was already an established and superbly skilled executive chef (and still only 25) when Meyer approached him with the opportunity to help build a restaurant and develop a completely new Nordic food concept. Redzepi was working at Copenhagen's prestigious Kong Hans Kælder restaurant at the time, but Meyer's offer of the role of head chef and co-owner of his new venture was too good to resist.

Established in 2004 and situated on the waterfront in Copenhagen harbour, in the once run-down but now very fashionable district of Christianshavn, the unusual restaurant was not a straightforward success at first. However, slowly but surely, it gained worldwide attention, gathering plaudits from respected critics all over the globe and two Michelin stars along the way.

There is no question that a sitting at Noma is something quite extraordinary. You will be served around 20 small plates of northern delicacies, which bear hardly any resemblance to anything you will have eaten before. On the menu you can find dishes such as Shrimp and Goosefoot, Radish and Yeast, Flower Tarts, Pickled and Smoked Quails' Eggs, Flatbread with Wild Roses, Caramelized Milk and Monkfish Liver, Burnt Leek and Cod Roe, as well as Beef Tartar and Ants, all served in ingeniously inventive ways.

For anyone who has had the pleasure of dining at Noma, it will be no surprise that it has been crowned The World's Best Restaurant by *Restaurant* magazine in 2010, 2011, 2012 and 2014.

SALMIAKKI

There are numerous varieties of liquorice claiming to be the world's best and most desired, but none of them stand a chance against Finnish *salmiakki*. With an intense, sweet and salty flavour that knocks you back if you're not familiar with it, one thing is for sure – you will never forget your first taste of this unique delicacy.

The hard, carbon-black, diamond-shaped *salmiakki* lozenge, which contains a relatively large amount of ammonium chloride, is admittedly an acquired taste. At first the combination was developed as cough medicine in the 18th century, but proved to be such a successful flavour that it was later produced as confectionery and its popularity rapidly spread across northern Europe.

Salmiakki was originally a trade name of the Finnish sweet manufacturer Fazer, but soon became a generic name for many varieties of this particularly potent type of liquorice. It is such a beloved flavour that the Finns also use *salmiakki* in cooking, especially in marinating meat, flavouring spirits, ice creams, breads, dips and sauces – and it is even used to create unusual cola drinks. A modern Finnish fashion brand devotes its entire collection to this delicious lozenge: you can find fantastic items – clutch bags, earrings, and necklaces – all in the unmistakable shape of the *salmiakki* diamond.

KANELBULLE

Although the Swedish cinnamon bun, or *kanelbulle*, could be considered a comparatively new addition to world of Scandinavian baking, it must be said that it is an imperative part of northern cuisine. The absence of these beauties would make for a very sad *fika* (coffee break) indeed.

One of the world's oldest spices, cinnamon found its way to Scandinavia through travelling merchants as early as the 14th century. However, for a long period it was mostly used for flavouring beer. The intensely fragrant spice cardamom was also introduced to the North around the same time.

In the 1920s, when sugar and flour became more widely available to the general Swedish population, housewives could allow themselves to start baking for pleasure rather than pure necessity – the unbeatable combination of cinnamon, cardamom, sugar and butter was discovered and the delicious scent of baking filled the houses.

It was in the 1960s, somewhere in Sweden, that a nifty housewife invented the typical look of the cinnamon bun – swirled into a sticky, sweet twist, brushed with a combination of whisked egg, a tiny pinch of salt and just a dash of water, then sprinkled with pearl-sugar (a type of sugar which doesn't melt even at high temperatures) and baked to perfection in a hot oven.

The *kanelbulle* was even awarded its very own national day in 1999: on 4 October, Scandinavians gather and celebrate the cinnamon bun, which has brought them all a little closer over a cup of coffee and a beloved sweet-treat break.

BOLLER

Apparently, the true origin of *boller* – Norway's most beloved buns, happily devoured at any time of day – is a mystery even to Norwegians. Nevertheless, according to the natives, eating one is a rite of passage and until you have done so you are not entitled to call yourself Norwegian. With various types, flavours and fillings on offer, one could even go so far as to say that *boller* are a way of life in Norway.

Like many Scandinavian cakes and buns, *boller* are not very sweet – just a touch of sugar is added to the mix. The basic dough is flavoured with cardamom, which provides a delicious platform for both sweet and savoury fillings. The buns, small enough to fit in the palm of your hand, were traditionally made with raisins, but nowadays many omit the raisins and enjoy plain *boller* with butter, chocolate spread, jam or other homemade preserves. We also have the schoolchildren's favourite: *skoleboller*, filled with vanilla custard, drowned in icing and topped off with heaps of toasted coconut. Savoury fillings can also be used, such as salami, cheese, coleslaw and cucumber.

You are free to adapt the basic recipe to invent your own type of *boller*. Some bakers make them with wholemeal flour and pulses to add fibre; others add cubes of Norwegian brown cheese or small pieces of smoked ham to the dough and sprinkle seeds on top before baking. You can even include your favourite spices and herbs to add more flavour – the options are endless. Find your own favourites and do as the Norwegians do: eat them for breakfast, lunch and supper!

SMÖRGÅSBORD

The origin of this world-famous phenomenon stems from the 14th century when the Swedish upper classes enjoyed snacks from the *brännvinsbord* – a smallish side table full of appetizers such as bread, butter, cheese, herring and plenty of alcoholic drinks (the word literally means 'brandy table') – before dinner. The custom grew in the mid-17th century when the table increased in size and moved from the side to the centre. This buffet-style service of both hot and cold food was particularly popular in railway stations and hotels as a main course for guests and travellers.

The 1912 Olympic Games were held in Stockholm, an event that put the term *smörgåsbord* (incorporating the word *smörgås* meaning 'open sandwich') firmly on the culinary map, with many restaurants emulating the style all over the world. In 1939, it garnered further international attention at the New York World's Fair, when a delicious *smörgåsbord* was offered on the menu at the Three Crown's Restaurant in the Swedish pavilion.

A successful *smörgåsbord*, put together in the correct way, is built up in five layers, much like a pyramid, with each layer representing a course. The meal is enjoyed in five separate servings and there are set rules and manners surrounding the devouring of the feast: the Swedes do like everything to run smoothly. It's a mortal sin to overload your plate and you'll be running the risk of getting barred if you do!

A proudly presented *smörgåsbord* would boast at least 60 dishes, plus a great variety of sauces and, of course, *brännvin*, the Swedes' breathtakingly strong brandy. Enjoy!

FÄVIKEN

There are plenty of fancy and expensive restaurants that the world could happily do without – but the tiny and exquisite Fäviken is not one of them. Making the trip to Magnus Nilsson's remarkable kitchen simply has to be on any person's bucket list.

Nilsson (born in 1983) is the man to see about a truly home-cooked Scandinavian meal. The restaurant lies deep in the inhospitable and rough terrain of Järpen in the Åre municipality, 750 km (460 miles) north of Stockholm, on the 8,000 hectare (20,000 acre) Fäviken estate. Since the restaurant opened in 2008, Nilsson has gained global respect and admiration for his relentless and innovative quest to live off the land and use seasonal produce in a traditional and eco-sensitive manner. All but very few ingredients are sourced – mainly by the head chef himself – from the vast farm on which the restaurant is situated or very close nearby from local suppliers.

The tiny restaurant seats only 16 people and, since the location is so remote, you will need to stay overnight to enjoy an authentically Scandinavian culinary experience. This is hardly a chore since the breathtaking views of the real and rugged North are worth the price alone.

The entire menu follows the seasons, and whatever Nilsson catches in the local pond becomes the true definition of 'fish of the day'. During the summer, the Fäviken foodstores are filled to the brim with fruit, vegetables, herbs and more, to see them through the isolating winter season. Vegetables are often served that have been cleverly stored for up to eight months!

Having been branded 'the world's most daring restaurant' by food critic Adam Sachs, and climbing the 'World's Best Restaurants' list to an impressive number 19 in 2014, Nilsson and his team deserve all the credit they get.

CHRISTMAS DECORATIONS

Up in the Nordic countries, we take handmade Christmas decorations very seriously indeed. Young and old gather at home to craft and chat; schools and social organizations go out of their way to invite both children and adults to an entire evening of creating Christmas together.

Anyone who has been invited to a Scandinavian home decorated for Christmas knows that there are very few sights that give you such a warm anticipation of the beckoning festivities. Scandinavians love candles of any kind, which is probably because of the long and very dark winter months. Every possible corner of the home has a lit candle in it, spreading a warm and comforting glow. Many children make their own wooden advent candleholders at school, and these sentimental creations are pulled out of storage every single Christmas – much to the embarrassment of the maker.

The Christmas tree simply has to be real pine, bedecked to the point of drooping with intricate straw decorations in the shapes of little angels, wreaths, hearts, goats and, of course, plenty of stars. Gingerbread biscuits are also a must in a Scandinavian Christmas home. They're even used as decorations, cut into different shapes – hearts, stars, reindeer – and threaded on a red ribbon, from which to hang them up in windows.

Every nook and cranny is decorated with white cut-out paper stars, little gnomes, Santas, toadstools, and beautifully homemade crackers. You simply can't beat a Scandinavian Christmas!

GLÖGG

The divine aroma of hot mulled wine meeting you in the doorway as you come in from a brisk walk in the crisp cold countryside is almost indescribable: the air is filled with the sweet scents of cloves, cinnamon, cardamom, ginger, orange and, of course, wine.

The tradition of drinking hot, sweet and spiced wine has its roots in Classical antiquity – the ancient Greeks and Romans were very fond of it and through southern European travellers it found its way to Scandinavia – where, unsurprisingly, it was welcomed with open arms.

In Sweden the name *glögg* was introduced in the early 1600s as a fitting name for the drink: the word *glödga* means 'to heat up until it glows'. The drink was produced by dousing a sugar cone in brandy, setting it alight and allowing the melted sugar to drip into red wine. Various spices were then added to create a breathtakingly powerful, hot, sweet drink. Mixed nuts and raisins were sometimes added for a bit of bite (or maybe just in an attempt to slow down the consumption a little...).

In the 1800s the popularity of the hot drink grew, with wine companies mass-producing ready mixed *glögg*. Sales soared during the cold winter season, which created a new, lasting association between the drink and Christmas. Nowadays you can find all kinds of *glögg* – strong, weak and non-alcoholic to suit all tastes, preferences and age groups – since there is nothing better than a steaming cup of hot, sweet wine, warming your ice-cold nose and hands in a Scandinavian winter!

CULTURAL
& NOIR
ICONS

GRETA GARBO

Greta Lovisa Gustafsson was born in Stockholm on 18 September 1905. She grew up to become one of the most iconic faces (and voices) in cinema history: Greta Garbo.

Young Greta was a shy but imaginative child, although she didn't enjoy studying and left school aged 13. She began working in a Stockholm department store and before long she was modelling hats for their catalogue, which led her to the more lucrative world of filmed advertising and acting.

In 1924, she played a major part in the film *Gösta Berlings Saga*, where she was spotted by movie mogul Louis B. Mayer (it was also around this time that she took on the surname Garbo, although the details behind the decision are a mystery). Struck by her intense magnetism, Meyer signed her to a contract with MGM and demanded she move to America. Her first English-speaking film, *The Torrent*, premiered in 1926 – both the film and its star were a big hit. Garbo went on to star in eight more silent movies before progressing to speaking parts in such classics as *Anna Christie*, *Queen Christina* and *Anna Karenina*. She was one of the most commercially successful actors of her generation and during her relatively brief career she was nominated for four Academy Awards for best actress.

Her final movie, *Two-Faced Woman*, opened in 1941. Having starred in 28 pictures between 1922 and 1941, Garbo left Hollywood behind for a life of simplicity and solitude, surrounding herself with a few trusted friends but often preferring to be left alone – 'drifting', as she said herself.

INGMAR BERGMAN

Ingmar Bergman (1918–2007) is, without doubt, Sweden's most celebrated film-maker. In a career spanning six decades he created thought-provoking and ground-breaking films such as *Wild Strawberries, Summer with Monika* and the Oscar-winning *Through a Glass Darkly, Cries and Whispers* and *Fanny and Alexander*. However, what most people immediately associate with Bergman is his harrowing choice of subject matter, such as illness, death, despair, unfaithfulness, betrayal, revenge, agony and insanity.

Bergman was born in Uppsala, just outside of Stockholm, in 1918. He and his two siblings were raised by very strict parents and his father, a Lutheran minister, regularly dealt out stern reprimands to the children. As an escape, Bergman developed a fascination for stories and acting, and created his own little stage for his marionettes. It was the only world in which the young boy felt entirely safe, understood and accepted.

Bergman was involved with the theatre in one way or another throughout his life, but it was in the world of cinema that he flourished most, and almost all his films were set in Sweden. His favourite place to shoot was Fårö, a small Baltic Sea island just north of the island of Gotland.

Bergman himself might have been an unsettled, contrary, insecure and complicated soul, but it was these characteristics that drove him to create the treasure trove of iconic Swedish movies and plays that we have today.

DOGME 95

'Basically, I'm afraid of everything in life, except film-making.' These are the insightful and frank words words of Danish film director and screenwriter Lars von Trier (born in 1956), whose work divides critics and audiences with its raw and complex approach to naked human emotions. As Hollywood was churning out blockbusters in the 1990s, von Trier and fellow Danish director Thomas Vinterberg (born in 1969) decided they'd had enough. Dogme 95 was formed in only 45 minutes, as Vinterberg and von Trier put together a manifesto – their 'Vow of Chastity'.

The ten rules of Dogme demanded that directors eschew any unnatural sound, light, props or other effects in their films. In essence, the manifesto states that the job of the director is not to try and shine through lavish effects but to have a script strong enough to carry itself with no post-production modification.

In 1998, Vinterberg's *Festen* (*The Celebration*) and von Trier's *Idioterne* (*The Idiots*) premiered at the Cannes Film Festival, where *Festen* was awarded the Jury Prize and the Dogme philosophy garnered much critical attention.

Even though the controversial cinematic movement ceased to exist in 2005, its original proponents are still producing challenging films and winning acclaim. Dogme 95 was created not to provide a low-budget option for film-makers, but to encourage a true movie-making process, which forces directors to use their imagination and to keep control over their own work. And, as von Trier himself opines, if you cannot keep control of your work, well, then – what's the point?

MADS MIKKELSEN

Women want to marry him, and many men would like to be him: we are of course talking about 'the sexiest man in the world', Danish actor Mads Mikkelsen. Maybe the clue to his success lies somewhat in his name – Mads is a Danish form of Matthew and means 'Gift of God'.

Mikkelsen (born in 1965) started out in life as a working-class child in Nørrebro, in the Osterbro area just north of Copenhagen city centre. As a youngster, he excelled at gymnastics and went on to become a professional dancer in Gothenburg, Sweden – a profession he was dedicated to for nearly a decade.

He did not start working as an actor until he was in his 30s, making his breakthrough playing Tonny in director Nicolas Winding Refn's film *Pusher* (1996), in which he appeared alongside Danish actor Kim Bodnia (see page 144). After this springboard role, Mikkelsen's career skyrocketed and he has since played numerous beautiful, unsettling, vulnerable and unforgettable characters, such as Stravinsky in *Coco Chanel & Igor Stravinsky* (2009), Johann Friedrich Struensee in *A Royal Affair* (2012), Jacob in *After the Wedding* (2006), Lucas in Thomas Vinterberg's Oscar-nominated *The Hunt* (2012), and of course the villainous Le Chiffre in the 21st James Bond movie, *Casino Royale* (2006).

Mikkelsen is a very active Goodwill Ambassador for the Danish non-profit organization 'Refunite', which is dedicated to developing and improving an online, mobile-enabled search tool, which aims to help reconnect as many as possible of the 43 million refugees displaced due to conflicts around the globe with their friends and families

LASSE HALLSTRÖM

The movies of Swedish director and screenwriter Lars Sven 'Lasse' Hallström distinguish themselves from other productions thanks to his calm, sensitive and amicable directing style – he simply waits and re-takes the scene until the actors have shaken off any self-consciousness that may hold them back, allowing the characters to emerge gradually and naturally.

Hallström was born in Stockholm in the summer of 1946, and, since times were hard for all of Scandinavia just after the war, with little or no money for toys, the young boy had to use his imagination when playing. He went on to study at the prestigious Adolf Fredrik's music school in Stockholm, but music was not Hallström's prime passion – it was film-making. His big break came in 1973 with a Swedish TV series called *Pappas Pojkar* (*Daddy's Boys*), and he also learned a lot about directing from making all but seven of ABBA's music videos.

After shooting a number of Swedish movies that garnered acclaim at international film festivals, Hallström made the moving coming-of-age film *My Life as a Dog* in 1985, which brought him global attention. He made his first American feature film, *Once Around*, in 1991 and went on to make numerous memorable films, including *The Cider House Rules*, *Chocolat*, *Salmon Fishing in the Yemen* and, most recently, *The Hundred-Foot Journey*. He is perhaps still best known for 1993's *What's Eating Gilbert Grape*, with standout performances from Johnny Depp and the Oscar-nominated Leonardo DiCaprio.

LUKAS MOODYSSON

To be named 'Sweden's most praised film-maker since Ingmar Bergman' by the _New York Times_, as Lukas Moodysson was, is a compliment any director in Scandinavia would happily give their right arm for.

Born in 1969, Moodysson grew up just outside Malmö in a home full of books – his mother is popular children's author Gull Åkerblom. Moodysson lived a fairly secluded life as a child and often felt like an outsider. He found a channel to express himself through poetry, and had his first collection published at the age of 17. By the time he was 23, he had released one novel and five volumes of poetry.

Almost everything Moodysson puts down on paper carries a lot of his personal experiences and personality, and, having decided that he needed to find a wider audience and create something less insular, he turned to cinema. He studied film-making at Sweden's Dramatiska Institutet (the only film school in the country at the time) and directed a few shorter pieces before he moved on to feature films.

A consistent thread in Moodysson's work is the need to expose people who abuse the weak and vulnerable in society; the compulsion to show that every action has a reaction. His breakthrough came in 1998, in the shape of the movie _Show Me Love_, depicting two teenage girls in northern rural Sweden, falling in love and experiencing all the awkwardness that comes with that time of life. Then in 2002 came _Lilya 4-ever_ about the life of an abandoned Russian girl. The 2009 film _Mammoth_ aroused much discussion about the horrors of human trafficking.

SARAH LUND
SOFIE GRÅBØL

Detective Sarah Lund, the central character in the Danish television series *Forbrydelsen* (better known to English-speaking audiences as *The Killing*), is in many ways a very evasive figure; the viewers gain little access to her feelings or opinions, and for a long time they are kept largely in the dark as to her private life and past. She dives headfirst into her police work, with little or no consideration for personal or professional consequences.

When thinking about how to play the role of Lund, created by writer Søren Sveistrup, actress Sofie Gråbøl realized that she had witnessed many of Lund's characteristics in the men that she knew, and so chose to model the detective accordingly, putting together the personality of the single-minded, investigator that audiences have come to love. A far easier task for Gråbøl, however, was being presented with suggestions for Lund's wardrobe before shooting. She immediately picked out a thick, woolly jumper with a fabulous Faroe Isle pattern by Guðrun & Guðrun (see page 90). And the rest, as they say, is history.

Born in Copenhagen in July 1968, Gråbøl was cast in her first movie at the tender age of 17 ('I thought it would be like a summer holiday job', she said later) after her mother had encouraged her to respond to a newspaper advert. Gråbøl's performance was noted and subsequently other offers for parts started coming in; without any formal training or theatrical education, all of a sudden, she found herself an actress and hasn't stopped working since.

LISBETH SALANDER
NOOMI RAPACE

Lisbeth Salander, alias 'Wasp', is a central character in Stieg Larsson's best-selling 'Millennium Trilogy' (see page 150). A 20-something computer hacker with a photographic memory and very poor social skills, Salander is extremely secretive about her past – the viewer is only afforded brief glimpses of her unsettled childhood. As a girl, she was deemed 'unsafe' because of frequent violent outbursts and was made a ward of the government after attempting to kill her own father for abusing her mother.

In Larsson's novels, Salander teams up with investigative journalist Mikael Blomkvist to solve a series of violent crimes. The books have sold more than 65 million copies, so bringing the character to life was an enormous challenge for the Swedish actor Noomi Rapace when she was cast in the role of Lisbeth Salander in 2009.

Rapace started acting at the age of eight, appearing in the Icelandic film *In the Shadow of the Raven* in 1988. Aged 15, she left her then home in Iceland and moved back to Sweden to study at a theatre school in Stockholm. She made her television debut in 1996 and has continued to receive outstanding reviews for her theatrical and screen performances ever since.

Rapace inhabits the character of Salander like a second skin; she even added real piercings to her face in order to become the perfect embodiment of the character. Between Larsson and Rapace, the personification of Salander shone a stark light on the physical, mental and sexual violence against many women in modern society.

KURT WALLANDER
KRISTER HENRIKSSON

Kurt Wallander is perhaps the first, and the greatest, hero of the Nordic Noir genre. The detective was created by award-winning crime writer Henning Mankell after his return to Sweden from a long stay in Africa. Taken aback by the growing segregation and racism in his homeland, Mankell was inspired to create his world-weary fighter for justice.

Wallander was given his very first case, *Mördare utan ansikte* (*Faceless Killers*), in 1991. The book was an instant hit in Sweden and nine more novels followed. To date, the Wallander books have been translated into 45 languages and sold 30 million copies worldwide.

Rolf Lassgård was the first to portray the detective on Swedish screens during the 1990s, but it was Krister Henriksson who really captured viewers' imaginations in adaptations made between 2005 and 2013. When trying to to convince Henriksson to take on the role, Mankell asked him if he had ever read any of the books. The actor replied in the negative and was duly given a copy... Henriksson soon found so many striking similarities between himself and Wallander that he wondered why he hadn't been asked to play him before. He characterizes Kurt as 'longing for something, but he doesn't know what it is' – a summary many of Mankell's readers would heartily agree with. Seeing the ease with which Henriksson inhabits the character of Wallander, one could almost say with conviction that if the two were to meet over a cup of coffee, they would have plenty to talk about.

THE LEGACY

To say that the new Danish television series *Arvingerne* ('The Heirs', titled *The Legacy* in English) was eagerly anticipated is an understatement – the rights to the entire series were snapped up by numerous countries around the world long before anyone had seen a single episode.

Arvingerne is written by Danish scriptwriter Maya Ilsøe and directed by Swedish actor and director Pernilla August. An array of Denmark's finest actors play the main characters in the series, which revolves around four siblings. The drama hinges on the death of their mother, Veronika Grønnegaard, an acclaimed artist who put her own creative hunger and desire for self-expression before the needs of her children. A wild child of the 1960s, eccentric Veronika left her children pretty much to fend for themselves, an abandonment that has had a profound impact on them and dominates how they lead their adult lives.

The series begin with Veronika's unexpected death, when it transpires that she has left her manor, Grønnegården, on the Danish island of Funen, to her daughter, Signe – much to the shock of her other children. Signe was given away for adoption and never knew her biological family, and havoc ensues among the remaining siblings as they unravel decades-old disputes caused by their mother's secrecy. The division of the estate forces Veronika's offspring into closer proximity than they might wish, compelling them to contemplate their own lives and acknowledge the very different adults they have become.

SAGA NORÉN AND MARTIN ROHDE
SOFIE HELIN AND KIM BODNIA

The first series of *The Bridge* burst on to Scandinavian TV screens in the autumn of 2011, with the gruesome discovery of a body intentionally left spanning the border between Sweden and Denmark on the Oresund Bridge (see page 161). Audiences were quickly captivated by the puzzling crime, but they were even more enchanted by Saga and Martin, the two wildly differing detectives forced to work together to solve the case.

Martin Rohde (played by Kim Bodnia) is a rugged yet charmingly emotional Danish detective who perhaps shares a few too many of the flaws of the criminals he hunts – he is willing to cut some corners if it gets results. His opposite number is Swedish detective Saga Norén (played by Sofia Helin), who is intense, by-the-book and highly intelligent, but almost completely socially unequipped. Saga is a direct and entirely unmasked persona, and while the production team has not confirmed it, the character shows signs of having some sort of disorder akin to Asperger syndrome, which makes her interaction with others fraught with difficulty.

The characters' relationship is non-sexual – perhaps more like that of a father and daughter – yet the collision of their professional styles and attitudes is extraordinarily compelling. Furthermore the tense drama unfolding on screen is expertly modulated by comic asides generated by Saga's awkward personality traits and Martin's futile attempts to teach her how to behave and react in a proper manner.

There are very few TV series that can boast having such an immediate impact on their viewers as the phenomenon that is *The Bridge*. Indeed, the first episode amassed over one million viewers when it was broadcast on UK television in 2012, a record number for any foreign-language drama.

BIRGITTE NYBORG
SIDSE BABETT KNUDSEN

A happily married woman with two children, Birgitte Nyborg has the same chores and commitments as any other working mother – but she also happens to be the political leader of Denmark. As the central character in the hit TV-series *Borgen*, Nyborg demonstrates the reality of a successful woman working in a male-dominated environment. The series goes behind the scenes of a public figure's life, devoting equal attention to Nyborg's home life and her day job in Christiansborg Palace (see page 162).

Despite the success of Scandinavian crime dramas such as *The Killing* (see page 138), Danish actor Sidse Babett Knudsen was a little taken aback when she was asked to play the lead in a new drama about a female politician's life. She assumed this was the last thing people would want to see, but the show's subsequent success proved her wrong.

Born in Copenhagen in 1968, Knudsen made her screen debut in 1997 in the comedy *Let's Get Lost*. Since then she has won numerous awards for her unforgettable performances in television, film and on the stage. While working on *Borgen*, Knudsen was very much involved in the shaping of Nyborg's character and was adamant that she had to be believable in all aspects: she had to project confidence and evoke trust and respect as a leader. The first series of *Borgen* aired in the autumn of 2010 in Denmark and was immediately embraced by its Danish audience. Soon, the English-speaking world got wind of it too, and it went on to find a global fan base.

ARNE DAHL

When asked why he chose to write crime novels, renowned Swedish author Arne Dahl simply responded: 'I write the books I want to read.' This straightforward and unpretentious philosophy can be observed throughout each of his nail-bitingly tense thrillers.

Today, Dahl is widely regarded as one of the very best crime writers in Scandinavia. His first series features the 'Intercrime' squad – a mixed bag of investigators brought together to solve a series of unusual and bloody crimes. The intense quest for answers is ostensibly led by troubled detective Paul Hjelm, but solving the cases frequently depends upon the diverse skills and individual strengths of the team. The novels are all based in Sweden, which, although not a country usually known for its crime statistics, reveals its darker side in Dahl's capable hands.

Dahl's second series of novels revolves around a controversial 'Opcop' team of Europol detectives. The group includes some of the old Intercrime detectives (the original band having been dissolved at the end of the first series), who have ventured outside Sweden to join a much larger European squad of investigators battling a vast arena of corruption, greed and evil.

As well as having a large audience among adults, Arne Dahl is also popular with a younger generation of readers and has written four far gentler crime books for children. In yet another twist, it has been revealed that Dahl is actually a pseudonym for the author Jan Arnald (born in 1963), the renowned Swedish novelist, literary critic and regular contributor to Swedish newspapers.

JO NESBØ

Norwegian Jo Nesbø is best known for his gritty series of crime novels set in the mean streets of Oslo and starring the damaged, alcoholic and demon-ridden detective, Harry Hole. *Flaggermusmannen* (*The Bat*) was published in Norway in 1997, and to date, nine more books have followed, with translations in countless languages.

Nesbø was born in 1960 in Molde, a city in the north of Norway. As a teenager, he had a promising career in front of him as a footballer, but he tore the cruciate ligaments in one of his knees at the age of 19 and had to rethink his future. Nesbø graduated with a degree in business administration and economics from the Norwegian School of Economics and became a stockbroker. By day he would sell stocks and shares, while by night he would write songs and perform with his brother in a rock band called Di Derre (meaning 'Those Guys' in Norwegian), which he still does today.

After having a hectic year in which he played 180 gigs with the band, while fully devoting his daytime to being a stockbroker, he found himself exhausted and close to a burnout, so decided to take some leave. Nesbø began writing his first novel featuring the discontented crime fighter on a plane flight to Australia in 1996, and the rest is history.

Nesbø also writes a children's book series about the crazy professor Doctor Proctor, a character who is very popular among young readers. In October 2013, it was revealed that Nesbø also writes under the pseudonym Tom Johansen, and has written at least three crime novels under that persona.

STIEG LARSSON

Stig-Erland Larsson (he later combined the two names to form Stieg) was born in 1954. He grew up in a very politically active family and displayed a strong passion for writing stories from an early age. When Larsson was 13, his father bought him a typewriter, although the incessant tapping meant he was soon relocated to the cellar to work.

Larsson always had an unquenchable need to uncover wrongdoing and suppression. He met his lifelong partner, Eva Gabrielsson, at an anti-Vietnam War protest and worked as correspondent for the UK magazine *Searchlight* fighting racism and fascism during the 1980s. Later he helped create the Expo Foundation, which concentrates on researching anti-Semitic organizations. As a result of his campaigning, Larsson was no stranger to harrassment and death threats. (Indeed, one reason why he and Eva never married was because it would have required them to declare their home address for the public record.)

In 1997, Larsson began writing his first novel, *Män som hatar kvinnor* ('Men Who Hate Women', later retitled *The Girl with the Dragon Tattoo*), planned as the first in a series of ten books. He was halfway through writing the third book when he signed a contract in 2003 with the publisher Norstedts for the rights to 'The Millennium Trilogy' (which also included *The Girl Who Played with Fire* and *The Girl Who Kicked the Hornet's Nest*). The three books follow the exploits of computer hacker Lisbeth Salander (see page 141) and the womanizing journalist Mikael Blomkvist. Despite their individual failings, together the unlikely companions form a brilliant crime-solving team.

Sadly, Larsson suffered a heart attack in 2004 and died just a few months before his first book was to be published, never seeing the worldwide success his novels were to achieve.

HENNING MANKELL

The bestselling author Henning Mankell describes himself as standing 'with one foot in the snow and one foot in the sand', because he divides his time between Sweden and Maputo in Mozambique and is very much at home in these two completely different continents, cultures and climates.

Mankell was born in 1948 in Stockholm, but grew up in Sveg, a small town in the north of Sweden where his father was a judge. Although his mother left and his father raised Mankell and his sister alone, he remembers his childhood as being a happy one. He recalls that as a boy, his favourite books were ones about Africa and he vowed to go there some day. Seeing his father at work also led Mankell to become interested in law enforcement and the quest for justice.

His first book, *Bergsprängaren* (*The Stone Blaster*), was published in 1973, and he wrote several more over the following years but the one that made his name was *Mördare utan ansikte* (*Faceless Killers*), published in Sweden in 1991, which was the first to feature the detective, Kurt Wallander (see page 142). The *Wallander* series has become a huge phenomenon, with numerous TV and film adaptations starring renowned actors such as Krister Henriksson, Rolf Lassgård and Kenneth Branagh.

Mankell has now closed his *Wallander* series, but he continues to write fiction and is also an active campaigner in bringing African issues to the attention of the West. In particular he has written widely and spoken frequently on the AIDS crisis that is devastating the continent.

CAMILLA LÄCKBERG

Camilla Läckberg has a distinct talent for exposing the dark underbelly of society. The main characters in her series of crime novels are policeman Patrik Hedström and author Erica Falck, who guide us through crime after crime, all the way to the bitter, and often bloody, conclusion.

When she was just five years old, Läckberg (born in 1974) began penning gruesome and intriguing tales. Her debut story, 'Tomten' ('Santa Claus'), showed early signs of Läckberg's nose for a thriller with Mrs Claus meeting a rather unfortunate end...

Läckberg grew up in a small seaside village called Fjällbacka on the west coast of Sweden, and it is here that almost all her novels take place. She stages startling murder cases in her childhood surroundings and weaves in local history and legends along with her profound love for the ocean.

Having completed her degree in economics at Gothenburg University, Läckberg took an evening class in crime-writing and went on to become Sweden's Queen of Crime. Her first novel, *Isprinsessan* (*The Ice Princess*) was published in 2003, and her eager fans have been seizing her novels from bookstore shelves ever since.

Läckberg is also a very busy businesswoman; to date she has published eight novels and is working on her ninth, she has produced two cookbooks, presented TV shows and is working on her third children's book. Added to all this, she is also an active ambassador for the Swedish Childhood Cancer Foundation and has co-founded Sahara, a silver jewellery business, with the designer Lovisa Wester.

KAY NIELSEN

With a father who was the managing director of the Dagmar Theatre in Copenhagen, and a celebrated actress for a mother, Danish illustrator Kay Nielsen (1886–1957) was destined to lead a creative life. He spent his childhood surrounded by props, costumes and charismatic actors, and he drew constantly.

After studying art in Paris from 1904 to 1911, Nielsen moved to England to seek work. In 1913, he received his first commission, to illustrate a collection of fairy-tales by Sir Arthur Quiller-Couch. His beautiful and intricate work soon brought him wide acclaim, and today his drawings are thought to epitomize the 'Golden Age of Illustration' alongside the likes of Arthur Rackham and Walter Crane.

In 1937 Nielsen began working as an illustrator for Walt Disney. His unmistakable work can be seen in two sequences for the animated epic *Fantasia*: the terrifying demons of 'Night on Bald Mountain' and the radiant sunrise accompanying 'Ave Maria'. Nielsen was a slow and meticulous worker, and as a result his time management clashed with Disney's approach to productivity and they let him go in 1941.

Nielsen never returned to Denmark and died almost penniless and forgotten at the age of 71; his home, clothing and food were provided by caring neighbours and friends. His work seemed destined to fade into obscurity, until the mid-1970s when publisher David Larkin issued a series of books filled with glorious works by artists and illustrators from the turn of the 20th century, and Nielsen's work once again found the acclaim it so richly deserves.

THE MOOMINS

An intriguing family of hippo-like creatures, the Moomins have charmed generations of young readers around the world. Their creator Tove Jansson encouraged her readers to trust and believe in themselves – to dare to ask questions and to reflect on their impact on and personal responsibility for their surroundings. 'Do not tire, never lose interest, never grow indifferent,' she said. 'Lose your invaluable curiosity and you let yourself die. It's as simple as that.'

Jansson was born in 1914, the oldest child in an artistic Swedish-speaking family in the Finnish capital Helsinki. A prolific and award-winning artist and author, she is best known for creating the various inhabitants of the Moomin Valley. Between 1945 and 1993, she wrote and illustrated nine Moomin storybooks, one comic-strip book and five picture books.

Inspired by Jansson's own family and friends, the main characters include the boyishly philosophical and adventurous Moominpappa; the worried and busy, but always in control Moominmamma; and the excitable Moomintroll himself, who gets into all sorts of trouble but tries so hard to be good. The Moomins are surrounded by a mix of sweet, scary, sad and witty characters, such as Moomintroll's friends Snufkin, Little My and the Snork Maiden.

The Moomins have appeared in numerous animated TV series and films over the years, as well as on a series of Finnish stamps. Since Tove's death in 2001 the Moomin legacy has been lovingly preserved by the Jansson family, and any Moomin-related product must be fully approved and endorsed by them.

LANDMARKS & ARCHITECTURE

ØRESUNDSBRON

The Oresund Bridge is one of the biggest infrastructures in Europe and constitutes half of the 16 km (10 mile) road-and-rail link between Denmark and Sweden. The massive bridge – 82,000 tonnes (90,000 tons) in weight – is a joy to cross since you can see for miles and miles as it stretches majestically over the Oresund strait. Outside Scandinavia people might be most familiar with the structure from the hit TV series *The Bridge* (see page 144), a popular crime drama that explored the cultural differences and similarities between the two neighbouring countries.

The idea to build a connection between Sweden and Denmark was already being voiced as early as 1872, when a tunnel was initially proposed. However, after a century of proposals, discussions and planning, the building of a bridge was finally agreed in 1991. The link was one of the most ambitious civil-engineering projects in the world, costing an estimated DKK 30 billion and requiring a massive team of designers, engineers and architects (the bridge itself was designed by architect Georg Rotne).

Construction began in 1993 and the final section of the bridge was set in place on 14 August 1999, when, as a symbol of unity, Sweden's Crown Princess Victoria and Denmark's Crown Prince Frederik walked towards each other on the bridge and met in the middle. Denmark's Queen Margrethe II and Sweden's King Carl XVI Gustaf inaugurated the crossing on 1 July 2000. Before the official opening, a few special 'bridge days' were held, during which thousands of people walked, ran or cycled across it. The official name given to the bridge is 'Øresundsbron', combining the Danish spelling of Øresund and the Swedish word *bron* (bridge).

CHRISTIANSBORG PALACE

The royal Danish castle Christiansborg Palace is the only building in the world to house all three governing powers under the same roof: the Royal Crown, the Supreme Court and the Danish Parliament. The Christiansborg Palace you can visit today rests on the foundations of several previous strongholds. The first castle was built on the site by Bishop Absalon of Roskilde in AD 1167. However, the castle's location on the tiny island of Slotsholmen was an obstacle to the trade routes and it was demolished stone by stone in 1369 by an irate Hanseatic League. A few years later yet another bishop felt the need for a palace of his own and built Copenhagen Castle, which was seized by King Eric VII in 1417, and since then the land and anything built on it belongs to the Crown.

The third castle, and the first one to be called Christiansborg, was built in 1746, but sadly it was almost completely ruined by fire in 1794. Number four was erected in 1828, but half a century later it was also destroyed by fire. The fifth attempt – the Royal Palace we admire today – was designed by architect Thorvald Jørgensen (1867–1946) and completed in 1928.

Just a handful of the things to see include the Royal Reception Rooms, the Great Hall with the Queen's Tapestries, the Royal Stables (including the massive indoor riding arena) and – not to be missed – you can see the ruins of Absalon's Castle and Copenhagen Castle deep underneath Christiansborg Palace and learn more about the 800-year-old history of all the castles that have stood on the site.

KRONBORG CASTLE

It is not entirely certain how William Shakespeare came to hear the story of Amleth, a ill-fated Danish prince, documented in the late 12th century by the historian Saxo Grammaticus, yet somehow he was inspired to write his own version of the sad tale, drawing on the fortress of Kronborg in Helsingør as his inspiration for Elsinore castle, the setting for his epic tragedy *Hamlet*.

Kronborg was built in the 1420s by King Eric of Pomerania on the extreme northeastern tip of Helsingør, stretching into the sea from Danish Zealand towards southern Sweden, which at the time belonged to Denmark. It was built as a stronghold for collecting valuable taxes from seafarers from all around the world who had to pass through this narrow sound between Sweden and Denmark.

The castle originally comprised a number of stone buildings and was surrounded by a square curtain wall, large portions of which are still part of the present day castle. However from 1574 to 1585, King Frederik II rebuilt the medieval castle in the Renaissance style of the time. The castle had soaring towers and lavish residential quarters for the king and queen, as well as an enormous banqueting hall, which at 62 m (68 yd) in length was the longest in the north at the time.

No doubt through stories relayed by travelling seafarers, Kronborg became a much talked about stronghold, and was well known throughout Europe for its magnificence and beauty.

TIVOLI GARDENS

When Danish army officer Georg Carstensen was persuading the reigning Danish king Christian VIII to allow him to create the Tivoli Gardens in the mid-18th century he declared: 'When people are amusing themselves, they do not think about politics'.

Considering that Copenhagen's Tivoli is the world's second oldest amusement park and is the second most popular seasonal theme park in the world, it's fair to say King Christian was right to grant Georg the five-year charter of the 6 hectares (15 acres) on which it still proudly stands. Today it covers a massive 8.5 hectares (21 acres) and uses every single inch to bring joy to the people. Come hail, rain, snow, sunshine, when you step through the impressive and majestic front arches of Copenhagen's Tivoli Gardens, all the worries of the world are left behind you.

Tivoli is a wonderland of things to see, hear, smell and experience: if you dare, you can hop on one of the world's oldest wooden rollercoasters, built 1914, which is still running today. The world's tallest carousel – the Star Flyer – is also housed at Tivoli: it lets you almost touch the sky with its tummy-swooping height of 80 m (260 ft) above the ground.

There is entertainment and care for both young and old in the shape of theatres, bandstands, restaurants, cafes, live music, carousels, lakes, fountains, animals, vintage cars, an aquarium, walkways, resting places, rides... With stunning flowerbeds themed according to the seasons it is an ever-evolving park, filled with influences from all over the world.

The most magical time in Tivoli is when darkness falls: an impressive 111,000 custom-designed lights are lit across the park. Additionally there's a weekly fireworks display on Saturday nights.

DJURGÅRDEN

Across three islands in the central Stockholm archipelago lies the popular Djurgården, which boasts over ten million visitors per year. Djurgården means 'game park', and the relatively small combined area of only 279 hectares (689 acres) of land and 183 hectares (452 acres) of surrounding waters was earmarked exclusively for royal hunting and leisure from the late Middle Ages. However from the mid-17th century onwards the local townsfolk were allowed to take walks there, have picnics and enjoy the many beautiful, unspoiled and ancient areas of the park.

Only a stone's throw from Stockholm's bustling city centre, Djurgården offers an abundance of recreational, educational and historical experiences: you can stroll along the 10 km (6 miles) of beaches, jump from the cliffs right into the ocean, peacefully canoe your way around the islands, walk through thick forests or enjoy untouched meadows – more than 800 types of plants and flowers grow in the park. If you're patient, you might also spy some of the park's 1,200 species of bugs and beetles.

Many of Stockholm's main attractions are to be found in Djurgården: four palaces, Stockholm University, Skansen (see page 179), foreign embassies, art galleries, the Vasa Museum (see page 16), the Nordic Museum, the ABBA Museum and the amusement park Gröna Lund. The park is very much a celebration of Swedish royal history, but it is also protector of northern Europe's largest collection of ancient oak trees – some as many as 500 years old and still standing strong. The largest one is said to be Prince Eugene's Oak Tree, which measures an impressive 9.2 m (30 ft) in circumference and could be up to 1,000 years old.

STAVE CHURCHES

Standing in front of a towering, timber-framed *stavkirke*, surrounded by the typical Norwegian landscape with its impressive mountains and sweeping fields, is an experience that no man or woman should miss: it is a truly moving and spiritual sight to behold.

Originating from medieval times – when the men of the north were terrorizing most of Europe – these astonishingly well-preserved stave churches can be found scattered all over Norway. Made entirely from Norwegian pine, the churches were built by local craftsmen as the Protestant faith spread through the country. However you cannot mistake the fact that it was Vikings who erected them. A typical stave church echoes the form of a traditional Viking longboat, the gables are often adorned with curious dragon heads and the buildings are decorated, inside and out, with elaborate and beautifully detailed carvings.

There are 28 stave churches remaining today, and one reason they have survived for so long is that all the outer wood was painted with several coats of dark-red tar, which has proven to be a highly effective preservative.

The word *stav* means 'staff' and relates to the buildings' structural cornerposts. The method of building these churches was called *reisvoerk*, meaning that the timber was laid vertically, instead of horizontally as was later the case. Skilled restoration work is continually required to preserve these wonderful places of sanctuary for centuries to come.

CHURCH OF HALLGRÍMUR

Hallgrímskirkja, with its tall steeple powerfully reaching up to the Nordic sky, is the true crown of Reykjavik in Iceland, and has become one of its best-known symbols.

In 1937, state architect Guðjón Samúelsson (1887–1950) was commissioned to create a place of peace and prayer for the people of the rapidly growing east side of Reykjavik. He found profound inspiration in Iceland's natural history and aimed to design the church in the image of the striking landscape surrounding him. Samúelsson's final, and perhaps greatest, architectural creation – he died before it was completed – reminds the viewer of the rough and rugged mountains, the tall smooth icecaps and the impressive lava formations that surround the island's active and inactive volcanoes.

Construction began in 1945, but the church did not open to the public until 1986. However it still lacked a church organ until 1992, when the German maker Johannes Klais delivered a 25-tonne (27.5-ton) instrument. One can only imagine the scratching of heads when the tedious work of assembling this grand piece started: it had 72 stops, 4 manuals and pedals and an impressive 5,275 pipes.

The church is named after Reverend Hallgrímur Pétursson (1614–74), Iceland's most beloved poet, who wrote the famous *Passíusálmar* ('Hymns of Passion'), which every Icelandic man, woman and child knows off by heart. In the top of the tall steeple, among a carillon of 29 smaller bells, there are 3 large ones, which honour Hallgrimur, his wife Guðrún and daughter Steinunn.

TEMPPELIAUKIO CHURCH

Imagine going for a stroll in the beautiful Finnish capital of Helsinki, only to stumble upon what appears to be a flying saucer that has crash-landed in the middle of a town square. That is exactly what the city's 'Rock Church' (as it is commonly known) looks like from a distance: it is embedded in a vast rocky outcrop, so the only thing you can see is a massive copper dome.

Plans for a special centre of worship on the site known as Temppeliaukio (Temple Square), where the church lies today, were in hand as early as 1930. At least two design competitions were held, but the onset of World War II meant that the idea was put on hold indefinitely. Finally, however, a third competition was held in 1961 and won by architect brothers Tuomo (1931–88) and Timo Suomalainen (born in 1928).

The church, which was built entirely underground, was quarried out of natural granite bedrock, created by blasting out the circular walls from the inside. An almost serene flood of natural light immerses the visitors through the 180 vertical glass panes upon which the domed copper ceiling rests. This dramatic combination of man-made and natural materials easily explains why this is one of Helsinki's most popular tourist attractions with up to 8,000 visitors per day during peak seasons.

The inner walls have been left fully uncovered, displaying the natural rock, as this provides excellent acoustics and creates a perfect arena for performing music. Every week, concerts are held in the church and during the Christmas holiday season you can enjoy them daily.

THE ARCTIC CATHEDRAL

Many have compared the Arctic Cathedral in Tromsø, the largest urban area in northern Norway, to Sydney Opera House and it is often referred to as 'the Opera House of Norway'. The stunning structure is visible as you fly into Tromsø airport, providing a striking first impression of the town. The building is, in fact, 'merely' a parish church, yet the remarkable architecture very much invites the viewer to use superlatives when describing it.

In 1960, the Norwegian architect Jan Inge Hovig (1920–77) began drawing drafts for the church that would become his most famous work. Ground was broken on 1 April 1964, and 19 months later, Bishop Monrad Norderval consecrated this astounding place of devotion.

The church is constructed from 11 cast-in-place aluminium-coated concrete lamella panels, laid out in a way that variously suggests an iceberg, boathouse or even a Sami tent. It comes as no surprise that Hovig said he was inspired by his northern heritage when designing the church.

Strips of light have been built in between the panels on the outside and the building is visible from all over Tromsø during the hours of darkness. The main entrance is a soaring wall of glass, which contains a large cross at its apex. The pews are of finest oak and the chandeliers made of Czech crystal hang from the ceiling in the shape of icicles. Behind the altar, on the eastern wall, is Europe's most extraordinary glass mosaic window, created by Norwegian artist Victor Sparre (1919–2008), depicting 'The Second Coming of Christ'. On bright days sunlight pours into the space through the window, making it look, quite literally, divine.

ALESUND

Fire, fire – everywhere there was fire! During the stormy night of 23 January 1904, a raging conflagration tore through the streets of the Norwegian town of Ålesund. The houses – typical of the time – were built entirely of wood and easily succumbed to the wind-driven flames. By morning the next day, 850 houses had been razed to the ground.

Incredibly, only one person perished in the fire, but 10,000 people found themselves homeless and penniless in the middle of a bitterly cold Norwegian winter. Before long, news of the fire spread to Europe, and Kaiser Wilhelm II, the last German Emperor and king of Prussia before the German monarchy was abolished, came to hear of the suffering of the Ålesund population. Wilhelm had spent many memorable holidays in the area and was moved by the news to send four warships filled with material and men to build temporary shelters for those left destitute by the fire.

Soon thereafter, discussions between 20 of Wilhelm's master builders and 30 Norwegian architects began as they drew up plans to rebuild the entire city. The architectural style in fashion at the time was Jugendstil, or Art Nouveau, and it was decided to build a brand new Ålesund in this elegant new manner.

The rebuilding of the town took just three years to finish and the romantic influence of Art Nouveau is unmistakeable with many of the buildings featuring colourful, swirling, organic ornamentation whilst others possess fantastic spires and turrets, or leafy wrought-iron balconies. The rebuilt city has become both nationally and internationally renowned as a remarkable snapshot of Art Nouveau design and architecture. If you visit, make sure you go to the Norwegian Centre of Art Nouveau Architecture, which suitably makes its home in Ålesund.

SUMMER HOUSES

In Swedish it is called a *sommar stuga*, in Norwegian *hytte*, Finnish *mökki*, Danish *sommerhus* and in Icelandic *sumarhús*. Whatever the language, the word summer house evokes memories of childhood, swimming in lakes, forests, mountains, eating outside in the sunshine, sitting chatting until it gets dark and hungry mosquitoes.

Industrialization arrived fairly late in Scandinavia, and many smaller cottages and farms were still in regular use until the 1940s and 1950s. It was only when the occupants moved into the cities around this time that they were transformed into summer houses or 'free-time houses'. In many cases, the houses had belonged to the same families for centuries; it is not common to sell off the property, but to keep it for the extended family to use as a welcome and calming break from the hustle and bustle of city life.

At the summer house, time seems to pass more slowly and life is to be enjoyed; many come with a bit of land and a few outhouses, so there is some manual labour to be done, but in a pleasant and peaceful way. The preferred way to travel is by bicycle; to cycle to the lake for an early morning or late evening skinny dip, or out to the main road to fetch the mail, visit the local convenience store or kiosk for a delicious ice cream, and then it's out into the back garden to pick some strawberries – quickly before your ice cream melts!

SKANSEN

A holiday in Sweden should absolutely include a visit to Skansen in Stockholm. It is the world's oldest open-air museum and is the proud host of Stockholm's only zoo, with an emphasis on Nordic animal heritage. There is so much to see and learn that you will need two days, if not more, to experience it all.

The museum's founder, Artur Hazelius (1833–1901), was a teacher, language enthusiast and educator who, during his travels around the Swedish kingdom, realized that traditional and ancient farming communities were about to disappear under the rolling wheels of the Industrial Revolution. In the spring of 1891, Hazelius was allowed to purchase a small piece of Skansen Mountain, on which he built replicas of old houses from different parts of Sweden to show the public. He was so productive that the park opened only a few months later, in autumn of that same year.

The main purpose of Skansen is to teach visitors how people lived and worked in all parts of Sweden through the centuries, including their clothing, buildings, food, occupations, animals and plants. This 'living museum' is filled with people dressed in period costume representing workers in different centuries, who will teach you all about themselves and their lives. Skansen is also the proud protector of about 150 original historic buildings, which have been moved to the grounds from all over Sweden. The only non-Swedish building is Vastveitloftet, a storehouse from Norway. Dating from the 14th century, it is also the oldest building on the site.

Skansen is located in Stockholm's Djurgården (see page 147) and visited by an impressive 1.4 million people a year, who enjoy all the open-air museum and zoo have to offer. Hazelius' motto was 'Know Yourself', because only through knowing your own history, will you get to know your own true self. And by building Skansen, he allowed others to do so.

LITTLE MERMAID (COPENHAGEN)

Whether in the refreshing rain of spring, the baking summer heat, howling autumn winds or the bitter northern winter chills, the Little Mermaid sits on her stone, longingly gazing at the world of humans.

Hans Christian Andersen's tale of yearning and belonging, *The Little Mermaid,* was first published in Denmark in 1837 and went on to become an incredibly popular fairy-tale for children all over the world. In 1909, Carl Jacobsen, son of the founder of the Carlsberg brewery, was so captivated by the story that he commissioned the Danish-Icelandic artist Edvard Eriksen (1876–1959) to create a sculpture of the little mermaid.

Eriksen decided to cast the figure in bronze and set her on a bed of large rocks, not too far out in the water at Copenhagen's Langelinie promenade. She took four years to finish and in 1913 she was ready to take her place in Danish waters where she belonged. The mermaid sits in a pensive posture, with her long hair swept over her shoulder on to her back. Her face was modelled after the Danish prima ballerina Ellen Price, but since she refused to model nude for the sculptor, Eriksen's wife Eline sat for the mermaid's body.

The Little Mermaid has since become a potent symbol for Danish nationalism and features frequently in tourist paraphernalia. Yet, the Little Mermaid continues to serve as a monument, recognizable to millions around the world, to one of Denmark's most famous sons.

DIRECTORY (STOCKISTS & ADDRESSES)

Bars and Cafés

101 Reykjavik
101reykjavik.co.uk

1 Kent Road
Southsea PO5 3EG
United Kingdom

Konditori
konditorinyc.com

182 Allen Street
New York, NY 10002
USA

Nordic Bakery
nordicbakery.com

14a Golden Square
London W1F 9JG
United Kingdom

37b New Cavendish Street
London W1G 8JR
United Kingdom

Nordic Bar
25 Newman Street
London W1T 1PN
United Kingdom

ScandiKitchen
scandikitchen.co.uk

61 Great Titchfield Street
London W1W 7PP
United Kingdom

Takk Coffee House
takkmcr.com

6 Tariff Street
Manchester M1 2FF
United Kingdom

Restaurants

Fäviken
faviken.com

Favikens Egendom AB
830 05 Jarpen
Sweden

Noma
noma.dk

Strandgade 93
1401 København K
Denmark

Fashion and Accessories

Acne Studios
acnestudios.com

Acne Studios flagship store
Norrmalmstorg 2
111 46 Stockholm
Sweden

Acne Studios, London
13 Dover Street
London W1S 4LN
United Kingdom

Acne Studios, New York
33 Greene Street
New York, NY 10013
USA

Gudrun & Gudrun
gudrungudrun.com

Flagship store
Niels Finsensgøta 13
100 Tórshavn
Faroe Islands

Hummel
hummel.net

Ilse Jacobsen
ilsejacobsen.com

Arne Jacobsens Alle 12
København K
2300 Copenhagen
Denmark

6 High Street
Tunbridge Wells
TN1 1UX
United Kindom

By Malene Birger
bymalenebirger.com

Copenhagen flagship store
Galleri K
Antonigade 10
1106 Copenhagen K
Denmark

By Malene Birger, London
28-29 Marylebone High
Street
London W1U 4PL
United Kingdom

Pia Wallén
piawallen.se

Studio Pia Wallén
Narvavagen 7
114 60 Stockholm
Sweden

Sandqvist
sandqvist.net

Swedenbogsgatan 3
SE-118 48
Stockholm

Swedish Hasbeens
swedishhasbeens.com

Flagship Store
Nytorgsgatan 36
Stockholm
Sweden

Design and Shopping

Alvar Aalto
alvaraalto.fi

Studio Aalto
Tiilimaki 20
0030 Helsinki

Finland

Arne Jacobsen
arne-jacobsen.com

Bang & Olufsen
bang-olufsen.com

Bang & Olufsen Center
Ostergade 18
Copenhagen 1100
Denmark

Bang & Olufsen of
Knightsbridge
3a, 50 Brompton Road
London SW3 1BW
United Kingdom

Bang & Olufsen of King
Street
4 Pall Mall
55 King Street
Manchester M2 4LQ
United Kingdom

Bang & Olufsen SoHo
63 Greene Street
New York, NY 10012
USA

Hus & Hem
husandhem.co.uk

The Design Quarter
12 High Street
Ledbury HR8 1DS
United Kingdom

Lego®
lego.com

The Lego® Store,
Copenhagen
Vimmelskaftet 37
1161 Kobenhavn K
Denmark

Louis Poulsen
louispoulsen.com

Lucie Kaas
luciekaas.com

Marimekko
marimekko.com

Marikmekko Helsinki
flagship store
Pohjoisesplanadi 33
00100 Helsinki
Finland

Marikmekko London store
16-17 St Christopher's Place
London W1U 1NZ
United Kingdom

Marikmekko NYC flagship
store
200 Fifth Avenue
New York, NY 10011
USA

Nord Design
nordesign.co.uk

5-7 Sussex Street
Cambridge CB1 1PA
United Kingdom

Scandinavia Design
scandinavia-design.fr

17 Le Prieure
49350 Saint-Georges-des-
Sept-Voies
France

Skandium
skandium.com

86 Marylebone High Street
London W1U 4QS
United Kingdom

245-249 Brompton Road
London SW3 2EP
United Kingdom

Tripp Trapp chair
stokke.com/TrippTrapp

Totally Swedish
totallyswedish.com

32 Crawford Street
London W1H 1LS
United Kingdom

Travel

Finnair
finnair.com

Icelandair
icelandair.com

Norwegian Airlines
norwegian.com

Organizations

Danish Church

5 St Katherine's Precinct
Regent's Park Outer Circle
London NW1 4HH
United Kingdom

Nordic Church and Cultural Centre

nordicliverpool.co.uk

138 Park Lane
Liverpool L1 8H
United Kingdom

Finnish Church

33 Albion Street
Rotherhithe
London SE16 7JG
United Kingdom

Swedish Church

6–11 Harcourt Street
London W1H 4AG
United Kingdom

The Danish Club

40 Dover Street
London W1X 3RB
United Kingdom

Embassy of Sweden

11 Montagu Place
London W1H 2AL
United Kingdom

Embassy of Iceland

2a Hans Street London
London SW1X 0JE
United Kingdom

Embassy of Finland

38 Chesham Place
London SW1X 8HW
United Kingdom

Finnish Institute

35–36 Eagle Street
London WC1R 4AQ
United Kingdom

Royal Danish Embassy

55 Sloane Street
London SW1X 9SR
United Kingdom

Royal Norwegian Embassy

25 Belgrave Square
London SW1X 8QD
United Kingdom

INDEX

PICTURE ACKNOWLEDGEMENTS

Alamy AF Archive 140, 145; Andrea Innocenti/CuboImages srl 166; Andreas von Einsiedel 81; Bygone Collection 31; Hipix 157; Inge Døskeland 65; Moviestore Collection Ltd. 139; Nils-Johan Norenlind/age fotostock Spain, S.L. 54; Photos12 146; Raga Jose Fuste/Prisma Bildagentur AG 17; Ragnar Th Sigurdsson/Arctic Images 18; Rainer Martini/LOOK Die Bildagentur der Fotografen GmbH 60; Ros Drinkwater 94; Sanna Lindberg/es-cuisine/PhotoAlto 105; Stuart Forster 87; Yadid Levy 164. **Bang & Olufsen** 82.
Bridgeman Images Victoria & Albert Museum, London 154. **Corbis** Robert Levin 78. **Courtesy of Malene Birger** A/S 97. **Fäviken** Erik Olsson 123.
Getty Images Anders Blomqvist 178; Desmond Morris Collection/UIG 25 left, 25 right; Fine Art Images/Heritage Images 20; Francois Durand 134; Silver Screen Collection 130; Tuul/hemis.fr 66. **Kakslauttanen Arctic Resort** 68.
Marimekko Corporation Helsinki-Helsingfors, design by Per-Olof Nyström for Marimekko 75. **Noma** Mikkel Heriba 115. **Press Association Images** Monica Schmidtz/TT News Agency 151. **Sandqvist** 99. **Shutterstock** Anton_Ivanov 42; Borisb17 180; Brykaylo Yuriy 175; Jamen Percy 45; kimson 160; Olga Miltsova 110; Robert Rozbora 48; vichie81 172.

ACKNOWLEDGEMENTS

The publishers would like to thank Jon Sadler at Arrow Films, Barry Forshaw, Kajsa Kinsella, Jane Ace, Cathy Heath and Anna Southgate for their contributions to this book.

Commissioning Editor Hannah Knowles

Project Editor Alex Stetter

Executive Art Editor Juliette Norsworthy

Designer and Illustrator Grace Helmer

Picture Researcher Jennifer Veall

Production Controller Sarah-Jayne Johnson

Text by Kajsa Kinsella